A short history
of the Netherlands

From prehistory
to the present day

The Golden Coach, a gift from the people of Amsterdam to Queen Wilhelmina on her ascension to the throne in 1898. It conveys the Royal Family to the Knights' Hall in The Hague on the third Tuesday in September when the new session of Parliament is opened

A short history of the Netherlands

From prehistory to the present day

by Prof. dr. P.J.A.N. Rietbergen

Third completely revised edition

BEKKING PUBLISHERS AMERSFOORT

Picture on cover: 'View of Delft'
Johannes Vermeer (1632-1675)
Mauritshuis The Hague

Third completely revised edition 1998.

Bekking Publishers Amersfoort
Postbus 286
3800 AG Amersfoort
The Netherlands

ISBN 90 6109 4402 NUGI 641

The Netherlands – a country of many waters ▶

Contents

◀ *The Netherlands – a country, won from the water*

A map of the Netherlands, showing the frontiers wrought by the fate of History

Introduction to the third, completely revised edition

The Netherlands as we now know it was moulded into its present shape over an immensely long period of time. Various elements were at work, both natural and artificial, including some of a political or military nature.
Long before man had ever won or lost territory by way of politics or military combat, he had experienced this at the hand of nature. There is no other European country in which nature, and especially water, has played such an important part as in the Netherlands. As a result the inhabitants soon devised ways to curb natural influences. The gap separating the men who first built mounds or 'terpen' along the coast of Friesland and Groningen over two thousands years ago from the designers of the recently-completed Delta Project, is not so wide as it seems. The need to control water was always foremost in the minds of the Dutch, then as it is now.

Some of these natural elements also gave the land its attraction. Situated opposite England on the Delta formed by the rivers Rhine, Maas and Scheldt, the Netherlands has commanded the major transport routes of Western Europe for thousands of years.
Therefor it is not surprising that this area has been a target of attack from all quarters since the beginning of history. The successive rulers known to us, the Romans, the Franks, the Burgundians and finally the Hapsburgs, have left their marks on the culture of the Netherlands. Many battles have been fought between the rulers of the various regions and against foreign invaders, to gain possession of the area and to defend or expand it. This explains the curiously erratic borders in the east and the south which can be seen on a contemporary map of the Netherlands. These were formed by chance front lines at the end of the numerous wars waged over the Netherlands, when areas were divided among the warring parties in the ensuing peace treaties.

This book gives an outline of the history of the Netherlands from prehistory until about 1450. The Burgundian-Hapsburg period, up till about 1550 is described in greater detail including the history of what is now Belgium. The struggle for independence of the Northern Netherlands (the country as it is today) in the sixteenth and seventeenth centuries, is described extensively as the period spans the birth and recognition of the sovereign state of the Netherlands. This is followed by the development of the Republic in the seventeenth and eighteenth centuries and the temporary loss if independence under French rule. Finally, the history of the Netherlands is recorded as from 1813, when present kingdom was established, until the present time

P.J. Rietbergen

Megalith graves near Havelte, built by the people of the 'funnel beaker culture' (Rijksmusem van Oudheden (RMO), Leiden)

Society, economy and culture during the prehistorical period – till 57 B.C.

The Ice Ages

During the time which, due to the absence of written sources, we call 'pre-history', the consecutive 'ice ages' or glacial periods determined the character of Northern Europe. Historical geography and paleo-biology yet can help us understand what the world looked like in those years. About 200,000 years ago, part of the present Netherlands was covered by a thick layer of ice. This penultimate glacial period lasted till c. 130.000 B.C. The ridges of hills to the north of the great rivers were formed when moraine was forced upwards by the ice. During the following millennia, when the northern polar cap started melting, the sea level rose and the valleys hollowed out by glaciers between the hills filled with water. Although the sea level at that time was about the same as it is today, the coastline was unrecognisable.
The ice did not reach the Netherlands again during the fourth and last ice age, which lasted until about 10,000 B.C.; yet, in that period the land was a desolate tundra.
The sea level began to rise again about 8000 B.C.; though by 5000 B.C. there were sea walls or dunes along what is now the North-Sea coast, large areas of the western Netherlands were flooded regularly, as is shown on the map; consequently, at the beginning of the christian era this part of the country was almost uninhabitable.

The earliest inhabitants

All that we now know of the earliest inhabitants of this country stems from archaeological finds, the product of chance and of systematic digs. Thus, the 1996 decision to construct a major railroad through the Netherlands connecting the coast with the German border offered a major opportunity for research into the early history of the area.
As far as we now know, people lived on the site of the present Utrecht hills as long ago as 150,000 B.C. They hunted big game such as reindeer and gathered fruit and nuts. Their primitive tools were made of flint and included the familiar stone axes.

The formation of the icecap drove these inhabitants away, and it seems it took a long time before human beings returned to this country. When they did so, in about 9000 B.C. they probably had no permanent settlements as yet; probably, they were nomads who wandered into the region in search of food.
There are traces of what may have been a campsite for huntsmen in North Brabant. The flint tools used by these hunters were much finer than those of the earliest inhabitants. Stone axes dating from about 7000 B.C. were found in the North Sea, halfway to England – by that time the North Sea was dry land, which only later was flooded over again.

These later inhabitants also lived on nuts and fruit as well as by hunting and fishing. However, new people arriving in about 6000 B.C. were farmers who probably also kept cattle – both agriculture and pastoralism having originated in the ancient Near East around 9000 B.C. They lived close together on a number of large farms in the south of Limburg, as well as on the high banks along the major rivers: they were the first people to settle permanently. They are known as 'band ceramists' because of the spiral design on their pottery. Like their hunting forebears, the 'band ceramists' still used implements made of flint. In Limburg flint mines were found which must have been in use for over five centuries.

The Funnel Beaker Culture and the Bell Beaker Culture

In addition to traces of their settlements and pottery, several of the burial places of the prehistoric inhabitants of the Netherlands can still be seen. The graves of the Funnel Beaker Folk are particularly impressive. These megalith tombs or barrows were built of huge boulders, first forced into this region by the ice; they were artificially arranged to form a vault, and originally covered with sand. The Funnel Beaker Folk were farmers and pastoralists, like the inhabitants of the sea walls along the coast of the North Sea and the river-country community known as the "Vlaardinger Civilization", whose houses have been discovered; the latter flourished between c. 3500 and 2500 B.C.

Traces of the Bell Beaker Folk, who lived between about 2500-2000 B.C., show that they had achieved an even higher level of technology. Excavations have revealed that they had mastered the technique of forging, using imported copper.
Also about this time, the first primitive agricultural implements came into use, including the plough. The first ploughs would only draw a furrow in light soil, but they were still a great improvement on tilling the land by hand. Improved agricultural methods led to the increased production of corn, which enabled the population to grow.

The Bronze Age

The period between 1900 and 750 B.C. is known as Europe's Bronze Age because utensils made of copper and of bronze – an alloy

Statuette found near Willemstad, in Zeeland, dated c. 5300 B.C. It probably was carved from a piece of soft oakwood by a hunter using a flint knife (R.M.O. Leiden)

of copper and tin – came into general use, marking another step forward in the field of technology.
This period was also saw the start of widespread trading on an international scale, as can be witnessed from some remarkable archaeological finds. A splendid bead necklace was excavated in Drenthe made of tin from Cornwall, amber – fossilized resin – from the Baltic and earthenware from Egypt, brought here either by the overland trading routes or by Mediterranean merchants.
Funeral rites changed at the end of the Bronze Age, which indicates a change in culture. The bodies of the dead were no longer buried but burnt, and urns containing the ashes were then put in special urnfields. Apparently, people now believed that the soul would survive, rather than the body. Funerary gifts buried with them suggest that in this period the inhabitants of the south of the country were of Celtic origin while those of the north belonged to the so-called Germanic peoples. Ultimately, however, they all descended from the tribes who originally had inhabited the region of southern Russia, northern Iraq and northern Iran; in periodic waves of migration, in the last millennia before the christian era they trecked to India and Persia as well as to central and western Europe. This common origin, which is most obvious in the various European languages, has caused these people to be named 'Indo-Europeans'. It goes to show that, given some time, anyone who arrived as foreign eventually will become indigenous.

The Iron Age

The production of iron, marking another change in technology, has been testified in the Netherlands from about 750 B.C. At this time, also, colonists left the safety of the high, but relatively sterile sandy soil of Drenthe for the fertile sea clay of Groningen and Friesland. They became cattle farmers,

Bronze torques, found in the marshes near Uddel; one of them is adorned with a piece of amber, that probably had been imported from the Baltic area (R.M.O. Leiden)

using the land for grazing; but because it was flooded regularly by the sea they constructed mounds on which to built their farmsteads. This seems to have been the earliest form of the Dutchmen's defence against the encroaching sea. Not satisfied with safeguarding themselves against the water, only, in later years they also succeeded in restraining the water and reclaiming land from the sea through the use of dikes, pumps, windmills and other techniques.

In the final centuries of the prehistoric period, tribes from the north of Europe succeeded in driving the Celts ever further to the South. At the beginning of the period staved by written records, the present Netherlands was populated mainly by Germanic tribes such as the Frisians in the north and the Batavians in the country along the great rivers. The Roman author Tacitus, using data provided by soldiers who had marched north to enlarge the realm of the Romans, describes the Germanic peoples as proud, touchy and warlike. Unlike people in the South, who inhabit closely built villages or cities, they prefer to keep a distance between their dwellings, built on artificial hills. They sacrifice to their gods in wooden temples, or just in the open air.

A bronze funeral urn dating form c. 700 B.C. and found near Oss. Besides the remains of a probably high-ranking person it contains a sword inlaid with gold, some bronze knives and pieces of clothing material (R.M.O. Leiden)

Society, economy and culture during the period of Roman rule (57 B.C. – 406 A.D.)

The first written text mentioning the Netherlands dates from 57 B.C. It is mainly concerned with the country at present known as Belgium. In this year, the armies of the Roman general Gaius Julius Caesar defeated the tribes living south of the Scheldt and Meuse rivers, such as the Eburons and the Menapians – groups who, at most, will have counted some 100.000 people. In his renowned "Commentarii de Bello Gallico" – the 'Comments on the War in Gaul' – Caesar describes the Celtic peoples in detail; this earliest record of the Netherlands later was used by such authors as Tacitus. It shows the Celtic civilization to have been quite splendid, as is confirmed by archaeological finds, such as the richly-ornamented bronze mirror found at Nijmegen, or the beautiful silver vase from Neerharen.

A unique silver vase found at Neerharen in 1831. It is embellished with geometrical motives, partly of Celtic origin. On the bottom is an illegible text, made up of Greek and Latin letters (R.M.O. Leiden.)

The influence of Roman culture

The advent of the Romans had far-reaching consequences for the lifestyle of the native tribes. Caesar and his successors decided to establish the frontier of the Roman Empire along the Rhine, consolidating it with a series of strategic, well-defended garrison camps, connected by roads which enabled the growth of trade as well as the advance of armies; Nijmegen was one of them – it is the place where a beautiful marble bust of Caesar has been found.
In addition to the network of roads which the Romans built when they settled permanently, they brought their culture – religion, language and everyday life – which now blended with Germanic customs, in some cases supplanting these altogether.
Temples were built, such as the one found in the village of Elst, in the Betuwe, now buried beneath the local Great Church – it shows the way in which the later Christians

Bronze masque, Roman, dating from A.D. 100, found at the fort near Leiden. This type was worn by the Roman cavalry during tournaments (R.M.O. Leiden)

were to celebrate their victory over the pagan religions. Beautiful villa's were constructed as the centre of great farming estates, their rooms decorated with colourful frescoes, and equipped with elaborate bathing facilities. Gold and silver jewellery and utensils were introduced. And the economy of the indigenous peoples, largely based on barter, now was influenced by the monetarized system of the Romans.
All this applied mainly to the Celtic-Germanic tribes living south of the great rivers. The Frisians who lived further north were never subjected to Roman rule although they were obliged to pay tribute for some time; this came to an end after an uprising in A.D.28. Yet even the northern Netherlands were influenced by the Romans, through their trade with the Roman garrison towns, which they supplied with corn and other foodstuffs, as well as with leather for shields and military clothing.

Artificial waterways

A few centuries earlier, native tribes had first built artificial barriers against the sea. Now the Romans set about constructing the first artificial waterways. One of the military commanders, Drusus, ordered a dam to be built near Cleves in 12 B.C., to ensure sufficient depth of the northern tributaries of the Rhine. He also had a canal dug to connect the Old Rhine to the river Vecht. Near the Roman "castellum" built there, a 25-metres long ship has been found recently, complete with a carpenter's kit. Around A.D. 50, the

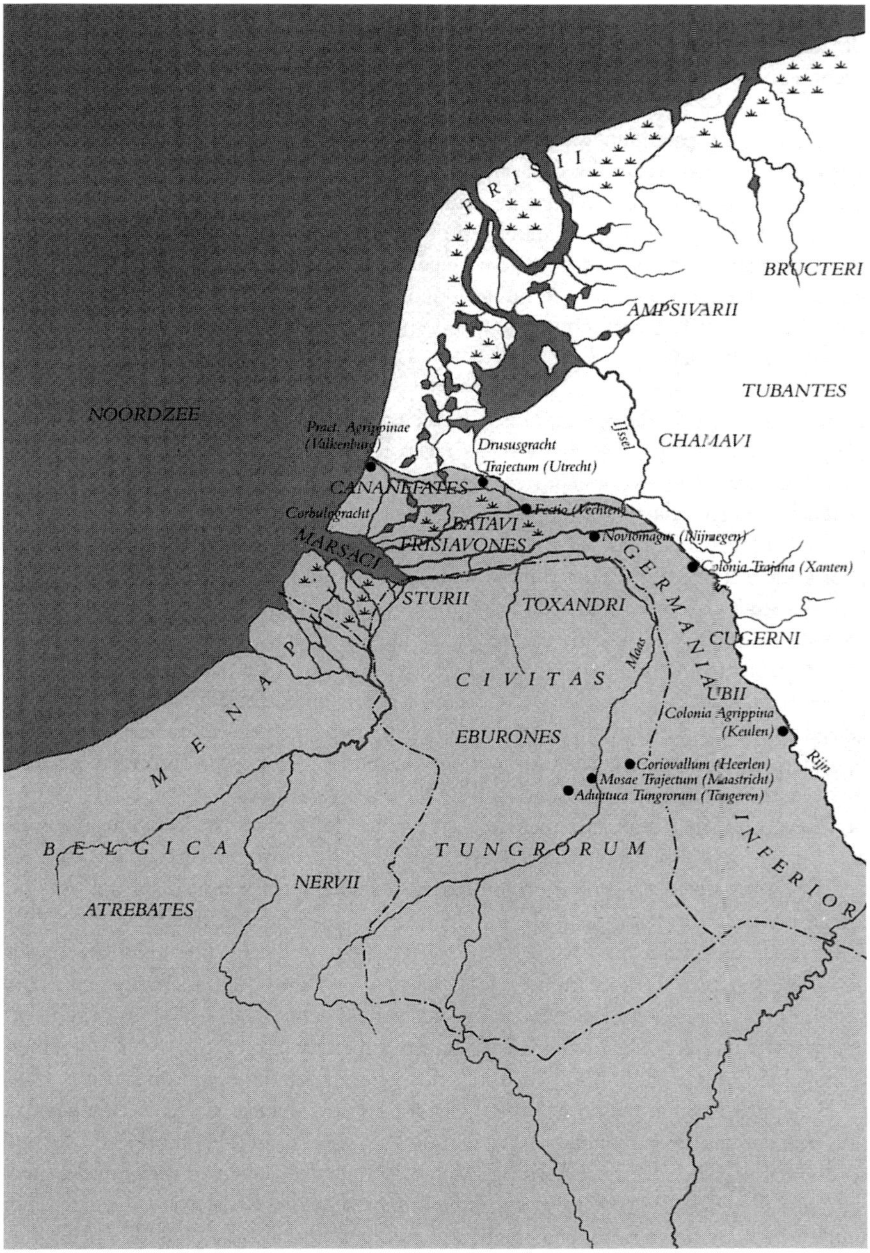

Map of the Netherlands during the early years of the Roman Empire

Roman commander Corbulo constructed a canal to connect the mouths of the Meuse and the Rhine The object of all these operations was to improve the passage to the northern parts of the Netherlands which had not yet been conquered.

But in the following centuries the water again defeated the inhabitants. The whole western part of the Netherlands became an almost uninhabitable peat bog which was inundated regularly by the sea. At the beginning of the era the land in the river basins around the mouths of the Rhine and Maas was quite densely populated. But by 300 the area was practically deserted.

This decline was partly caused by the decline of Roman power and authority. Forced by problems in the Roman heartland, the Roman troops gradually left these regions. The military commanders in Rome, continually contesting for dominion during the third century, had little thought for what went on in the outposts of the Empire. Formerly, efficient administrative units had been formed by dividing the area into two provinces, subdivided into *'civitates'*, urban centres of regional government, backed by the legions that turned authority into power. Now, central government was increasingly less effective; consequently, the organization of labour necessary to keep all these waterworks properly functioning posed a problem; in the end, the system simply failed. Also, the northern borders now became vulnerable to attack, mainly from Germanic tribes who, in waves of migration from central and eastern Europe, tried to enter the more prosperous border regions of the Empire.

According to tradition, Roman rule in the Netherlands finally came to an end in 406, when the Romans were forced to surrender the series of forts they had constructed to reinforce the natural boundary formed by the Rhine.

Silver-and-gilt helmet from the 4th century, discovered in the marshes of the Peel, where its owner, a Roman officer, found his death (R.M.O. Leiden)

Society and economy in the Germanic world, up till c. 750 A.D.

A great deal of the cultural influence of the Romans disappeared when they withdrew from these parts; Germanic culture once more took its place.
Economically speaking, Germanic society was rather more primitive than Roman civilization, as it was based on agriculture, only. Politically, society was less complex, too. However, from the basic family- and clan-structures slowly larger units emerged, with a tribal structure. These mostly were led by the priests, by chieftains or kings and, in times of trouble, by army leaders, the latter probably chosen from among the bravest men of the tribe.
In the course of the third century, a number of smaller Germanic war bands and tribes united to form larger communities. Gradually, two groups emerged, the Saxons and the Franks; to the north of their home lands, the Frisians maintained their position. The land was divided into shires headed by a sheriff of the tribunal and an officer of the king. From the sixth century onwards these offices were usually held by one person.

The Crown and the Estates

Germanic kingdoms and their form of kingship bore no resemblance to the institutions of the same name in our day and age. The Germanic kingdom was not lasting, either in time or place. Kings were chosen at a tribal meeting of free and able-bodied men. Sometimes kingship was the prerogative of members of a particular family, who boasted their descent from a famous, heroic, or even semi-divine ancestor, but even so it existed by the grace of the people.
The main concern of the king was to take care of affairs involving the worlds of both gods and men, co-operating with the priests, the druids. In time of war he usually led the army, though others were sometimes chosen for this task, if they showed greater military ability. He had no say in internal affairs such as the local administration of justice. These were dealt with by the local communities themselves.
Socially, the Germanic peoples were divided into four estates; the nobility (not hereditary among the Franks), descending from those who had gained their landed property in reward for outstanding military exploits, the thanes or free-born men, the freedmen and the serfs. Only the men from the two upper estates had the right to take part in tribal meetings, which, however, were not convened regularly.

The Saxons, the Frisians and the Franks

The Germanic Saxons lived mainly in the east of the Netherlands. But the centre of their power lay east of the great Dutch rivers, in what is now Germany.

The Frisians were descendants of the colonists who originally had left the barren sandy soil of Drenthe and had survived on their mounds for centuries. Already during the Roman period, they were engaged in extensive trading, bartering their own produce including cattle, hides and wool in exchange for luxury goods, or occasionally for money. In this way the mound dwellers of the fourth and fifth centuries had achieved a high standard of civilization in comparison with the inhabitants of the rest of the country. They were able to militarily expand their power and subsequently populate the land southwards as far as the great rivers, even reaching Flanders along the coast. They traded the so-called Frisian cloth famous across the whole of north-western Europe, but there is some doubt as to whether it was actually made in Friesland,

Frankish 'fibula': a bronze clasp in the form of a bird, set with an almandine. This jewel belonged to a woman of the 5th century, living near Gennep (R.M.O. Leiden)

or bought by them in Flanders and then distributed under their own name.

The Franks who had settled to the south of the great rivers had conquered extensive territories during the centuries following the withdrawal of the Romans. From his base in present-day Belgium, Clovis, or Chlodwig I, of the Merovingian dynasty and king of the Franks from 481-511, waged numerous wars to gain dominion over the whole of Gaul, known to us today as France and northern Italy; he also ruled over the Netherlands as far as the Rhine: a Merovingian settlement has been found near the remains of the Roman fortress at Nijmegen. After Clovis's death, the kingdom of the Franks was divided among his four sons who were expected to co-operate closely. Theodoric I ruled the part which included the southern Netherlands, called Austrasia.
Meanwhile, the Frankish nobles, relying on their military might, became increasingly independent. This applied especially to the master of the royal household or chamberlain. From the seventh century onwards, these chamberlains, from the family of the Carolingians or Pippinids held the actual power in the Frankish kingdom. Yet even they could not do without the support of the regional magnates.

Culture in the Germanic world: paganism and conversion to Christianity

The world of the Germanic gods

Archaeology as well as such descriptions as the ones left by Caesar and Tacitus show that the Germanic people believed in the divine power of all natural forces. From their own everyday experiences with nature's many incomprehensible forces, they created an imaginary world and peopled it with gods who personified and hence controlled these forces. The mightiest of these was Wodan, victor in battle and ancestor of all royal families: by extending their genealogies backwards to include these gods, the chieftains legitimized their authority.
Another powerful god was Donar, who governed the clouds and the rain, the thunder and the lightning; these powers made him very important to the farming community. There was also Freya, the goddess of love and fertility. These and numerous minor deities, often locally different, influenced the little things of everyday life for better or worse.
The gods were worshipped in nature, at places which were awe-inspiring in themselves, for instance by a great old tree, or on a hilltop. Simple wooden temples also were built. Sacrifices were made on an altar within an enclosure; typically, tribal meetings were held there, too, giving the decisions in matters political, which mostly meant military, a hallowed atmosphere.

Conversion to Christianity under the Frankish rulers

Christianity, which had spread from the Near East over the Roman Empire during the second and third centuries A.D., already had gained some following in the romanized parts of the Netherlands in the fourth century. There is a record stating that Gervase, bishop of Tongeren, took part in the synods of bishops in AD 343 and 359. The same Gervase later moved his see from Tongeren to Maastricht. According to legend he lies buried where the great church of St. Gervase still stands today.

The real breakthrough for Christianity came with the baptism of the Frankish king Clovis I, the head of a romanized tribe, at the beginning of the sixth century. According to legend, he pledged himself to the christian God in the heat of battle against a Germanic enemy. Obviously, this baptism also was politically motivated. There were many Christians in the originally Roman towns and villages of the Frankish empire, and their efficient episcopal organization was a desirable source of power and authority to the king.
With the aid of the Frankish rulers, conversion to Christianity of the entire region south of the great rivers was almost complete by 700, but the Germanic religion was still observed in the north.
There, the Frisians persisted in their ancestral beliefs although a small Christian church had been established at Utrecht in 630. Possibly, they mistrusted the missionaries who came to convert them with the support of the Frankish rulers, viewing them as advance troops of the enemy. It was only when preachers from Ireland and England, which had been christianized already, came to visit the Frisians that their conversion took hold. The first of these preachers was bishop Wilfred. Driven ashore on the Frisian coast while on his way to Rome, Wilfred was made welcome by king Aldgillis. He was able to preach the gospel in Friesland during the entire winter of 678.

Willibrord and Boniface

In 695, Pope Sergius I consecrated the Anglo-Saxon monk Willibrord bishop of the Frisians, at that time temporarily under Frankish rule. Willibrord took up residence in the old mission post at Utrecht where he founded the churches of Saint Martin and Saint Salvator. However, Willibrord was obliged to withdraw from Utrecht when the Frisian king Radbod drove out the Franks in 714.

After successful mission work in the German lands, the monk Boniface, in his old age, wanted to prove his worth with the hostile and headstrong Frisians. However, he was not prepared to bring the gospel to Friesland until Willibrord had returned to Utrecht. This took place in 734, the year in which Friesland was finally annexed to the Frankish empire after being defeated by the royal chamberlain Charles Martel. Yet not all Frisians welcomed Boniface's efforts, as is shown by his murder near Dokkum in 754; the old religion continued to flourish for some time to come.

Early-Christian tombstone, from the churchyard of the great basilica of St.Gervase at Maastricht, probably dating from the 5th century (R.M.O. Leiden)

Society, politics, economy and culture in the Carolingian Empire (c. 650-850)

The Frankish empire expands

For centuries, the great rivers had served as a natural boundary for the domains of the south, first the Roman Empire and later the Frankish realm. The Romans had built a number of military forts along the Rhine. At one of these – fort Levefanum – a trading centre sprang up during the seventh century called Dorestad, near the present site of Wijk bij Duurstede. This trading centre was of great importance to both the Frisians and the Franks as it dominated trade in the whole of north-western Europe; it was a central market on a route connecting the Frankish economy and the Mediterranean with the Baltic Sea, and the trade of Russia, and even the empire of the islamic khalifs in Baghdad. Along this route, supplies of silver, essential to the economy of western Europe, came to Dorestad via Russia and Persia, amber, furs and corn came from the Baltic shores, wine came from France, and even exotic produce from Africa reached Dorestad.
Fierce fighting ensued over this place. In 689, the Frankish chamberlain Pippin II defeated the Frisian king Radboud at Dorestad. After Pippin's death, Radbod succeeded in recovering the territory won by the Franks. Meanwhile, the rule of the Frisian kings was drawing to a close. In 734, the Frisian military commander Bubo was defeated by the Frankish chamberlain Charles Martel, who now extended the Frankish kingdom to the 'Lauwers' Sea and the North Sea.

From chamberlains to kings: the Carolingians

Charles's son Pippin III proclaimed himself king of the Franks after deposing the last Merovingian ruler. He was anointed by the missionary Boniface to demonstrate that his kingship was of a different nature from that of the primitive Germanic rulers. He consciously placed himself in the tradition of the Roman-imperial line and of the jewish-christian rulers, annointed by God's priests. In this way the Crown gained a new dignity derived from imperial Rome and from the Old Testament, raising it above the simple authority of former days.

The Emperor Charlemagne (800-814)

Pippin III died in 768. He was succeeded by his two sons, one of whom died only three years later. Charles, the remaining son, then became the absolute monarch, later known to the people as Charlemagne. He campaigned relentlessly against the Saxons, who threatened the north-western frontier of the Frankish realm. Following a decisive victory over them in 785, his rule was accepted in these parts.
Even more than his father, Charlemagne saw himself as the lawful successor to the Roman emperors whose rule he wanted to re-establish. For this reason, in AD 800 he went to Rome, to be crowned there by the pope.
The empire had no specific capital. Charlemagne often held court at Aachen, but he also paid regular visits to the outposts of his territories. He sometimes stayed in the Netherlands, where he had a palace-castle at Nijmegen.

The realm of Charlemagne was administered by civil servants, or counts in charge of the counties. The names of several of these counties have survived in the present Netherlands, as in Twente, Batua (Betuwe), Gooi and Brabant. The main task of Carolingian counts was to administer justice at the head of a tribunal of freemen, the aldermen. In order to control these counts, who, due to defective communications in this vast empire, could easily become too independent, the Emperor used to send confidants to spy on them.

The feudal system as instrument of administration

Though the Frankish empire was an important state, especially in the times of the first Carolingians, the power of the ruler, of central authority, was definitely little if compared to present-day norms. Necessarily, rulers surrounded themselves with a number of trusted relatives or servants. First of all, they could not personally govern the entire realm; nor could they base their administration on written orders, only: as most people were illiterate, authority had to be exercised personally, and locally. Consequently, most princes felt forced to delegate the exercise of certain sovereign rights, in the field of justice and taxation but also in matters military, to regional magnates, the great landowners. These high 'officials' often were rewarded with even more land, as well as with specific privileges. Those who followed and helped them also were given land. However, officially these grants were not made to be freely held in perpetuity, but for a specific period, only; these 'fiefs' – hence: the feudal system – were seen as the return for services to the Crown, which had to be rendered continually. The system was flexible: even those who lost their land to a Frankish king in combat were allowed to hold their land in fee. In exchange they had to acknowledge Frankish sovereignty.

The feudal system and large-scale landownership; a new class: the villeins

Agriculture and livestock were still the main sources of livelihood in Carolingian times. But the rise of feudalism brought considerable changes in economic and social organization. Previously rare, large-scale landownership became the rule now, especially in the south. This resulted in a new class of people, the villeins, who were granted a piece of land for their own use, but who were also obliged to cultivate the land belonging to their landlord. The partial disappearance of a money-based economy, caused by the decline of the import of precious metal from the Mediterranean south and the Near East between the third and the seventh century, also played a part in this reversion to an agricultural economy. Payments were usually made in kind and by means of personal services.

Trade flourishes

The organizational structure of the Carologina empire guaranteed a certain

Equestrian statue of the Emperor Charlemagne (800-816)

freedom and safety of communication over a large area; consequently, from the seventh century onward, trade, in addition to agriculture, became important once more as a means to providing a livelihood. As boundaries shifted to the north under Carolingian rule, this led to brisk trading in Northwest Europe during the eighth and ninth centuries, bringing prosperity to the entire empire.

In this, the Frisians playing a leading part. During this period, the old trading centre of Dorestad grew to become the foremost Frisian trading town. However, in the course of the ninth century this flourishing city suffered many attacks at the hands of the so-called Norsemen. Also, though it is likely that the city's harbour was already falling into disuse when the Rhine slowly shifted its bed. Besides Dorestad, Medemblik and Stavoren, both situated on the shores of the great Almere (the later Zuiderzee, and now the IJsselmeer) and thus connected to the North Sea and international trade, were important commercial centres as well.

A Carolingian renaissance?

At the court of Charlemagne and his successors, there was a marked revival of interest in ancient Roman and Greek culture; this process has been described as the Carolingian 'renaissance'. Many a classic text was saved for posterity during the Carolingian period by the monks' zeal; for it was especially the monasteries which held alive a tradition of Latin scholarship and culture, mainly in the fields of philosophy, literature and the arts. However, the leaders of the Church were not specifically interested in the culture of ancient Rome for itself; rather, they wanted to preserve those elements that could be used to provide the christian-Carolingian empire with a strong, well-educated elite.

It is said that Charlemagne, always eager to learn, studied Latin late in life. He also promoted education for the future leadership of his state. The Church was to provide this education on a classical basis. The subjects that were taught were called the seven liberal arts. The 'trivium', consisting of grammar, rhetoric and logic, was taught to younger pupils, while the 'quadrivium', for more advanced pupils, consisted of four subjects: geometry, astronomy, arithmetic and music. In reality this education was reserved for a select few, mainly prospective clergy and members of the nobility. Lessons were exclusively given at court, or in monasteries and in the schools attached to cathedrals. The schools in Utrecht belonging to the churches of Saint Martin and Saint Salvator became renowned. Future clergy from the whole of the northern Frankish empire were sent to these schools.

Charlemagne also stimulated musical education. He founded a choir school at Metz, and by introducing the Gregorian plainsong hymnal he succeeded in persuading the clergy to introduce hymn-singing during church services.

The division of the Carolingian empire

On his death in 814, Charlemagne was succeeded by his son Louis the Pious. At the Treaty of Verdun in 843 the empire was divided among Louis' three sons. Lothair inherited the central part, including the region later to be known as the Netherlands, and with it the imperial crown.

On the death of Lothair in 855, the central empire was again divided, once more into three parts, with the Netherlands in the northernmost part, called Lorraine.

Following various other divisions and annexations to East and West Frankland, Henry I, king of Germany, in 925 succeeded in subjecting Lorraine, and the Netherlands, to his rule. Officially, the Netherlands were to remain part of the so-called Holy Roman Empire until 1648, but actual power soon lay elsewhere: not with the 'German' emperors, but with regional princes, who

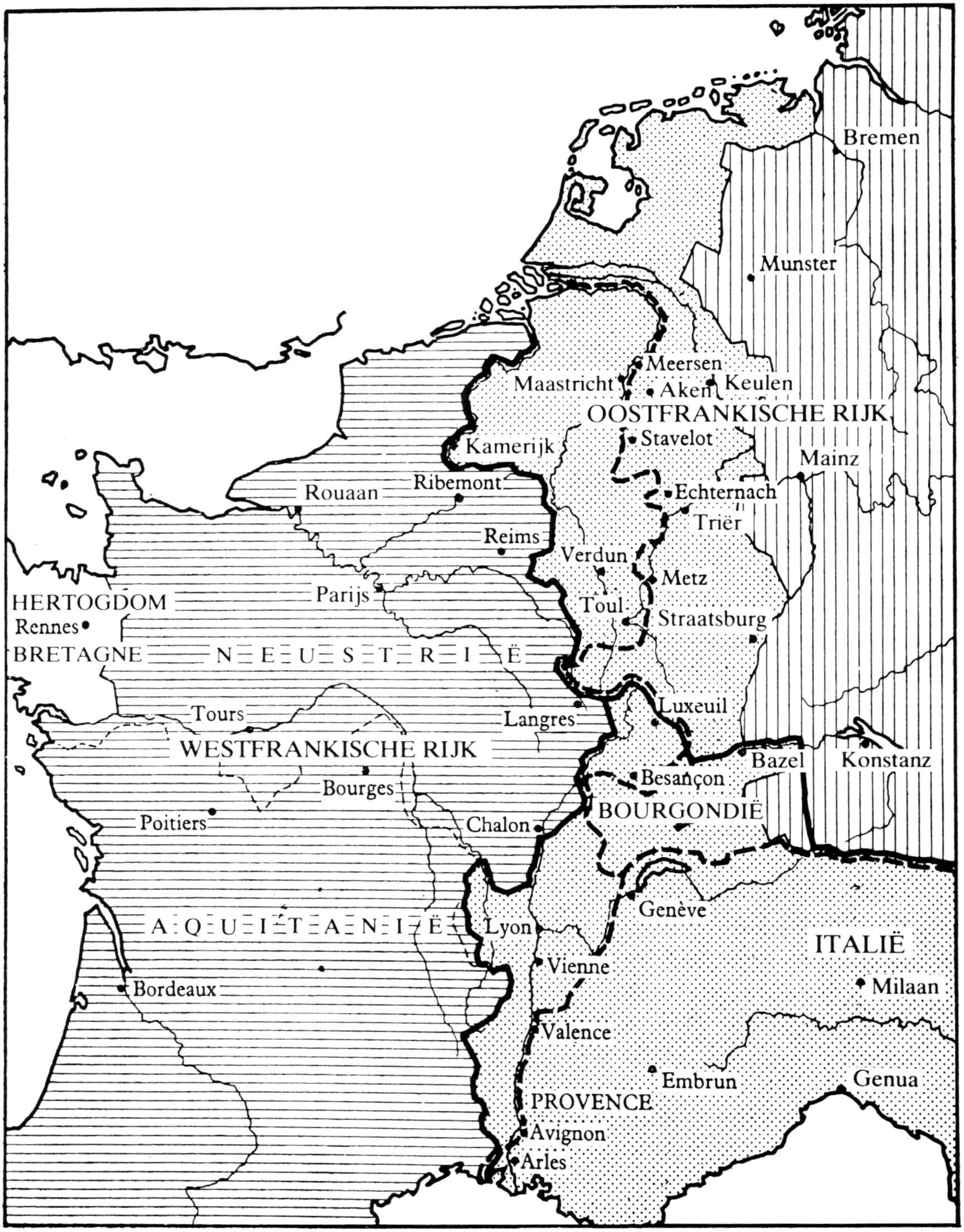
Bremen
Munster
Meersen
Maastricht
Aken
Keulen
OOSTFRANKISCHE RIJK
Stavelot
Mainz
Kamerijk
Rouaan
Ribemont
Echternach
Trier
Reims
Verdun
Metz
Parijs
Toul
Straatsburg
HERTOGDOM
Rennes
BRETAGNE
N E U S T R I Ë
Tours
Langres
Luxeuil
WESTFRANKISCHE RIJK
Bazel
Konstanz
Besançon
Bourges
BOURGONDIË
Poitiers
Chalon
Genève
A Q U I T A N I Ë
Lyon
ITALIË
Vienne
Milaan
Bordeaux
Valence
Embrun
Genua
PROVENCE
Avignon
Arles

increasingly separated themselves from the central sovereign power. Indeed, with the weakening of central authority after Charlemagne's death, the major regional magnates became virtually independent. The invasions of the Norsemen or Vikings between 800 and 1000 and the ensuing chaos certainly caused many to entrust their land to powerful rulers – the old princes, insofar as they succeeded in offering their protective services, but also new men, and even the Church, which had grown rich and powerful as well. In order to receive protection, and on condition that one rendered military service to one's liege lord, one received one's land back in fief.

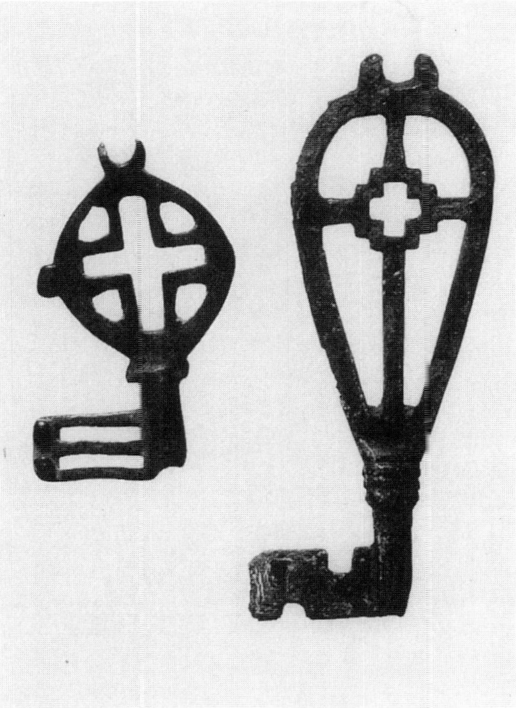

Bronze keys from the 8th century, found in Dorestad. After the introduction of Christianity in the northern Netherlands, keys often were adorned with complex cruciform elements (R.M.O. Leiden)

Division of the Carolingian Empire in the Treaty of Verdun, of 843

the western empire of Charles the Bold

the central empire of Lothair

the eastern empire of Louis the German

A gold, gem-set brooch, c. 800 A.D., found in Dorestad. It is inlaid with enamel, coloured glass, semi-precious stones and small pearls, in such a way that not only two crosses are formed but also, with the help of gold thread, trees of life and birds, both referring to Paradise. The jewel obviously belonged to a Church dignitary (R.M.O. Leiden)

The raids of the Norsemen, c. 850-1000

The name Norseman or Viking does not denote any specific ethnic group; they were the names given to inhabitants of the Nordic countries we now know as Denmark, Norway and Sweden, between about 850 and 1000. In the far, cold north, these peoples lived precariously on agriculture, fishery and hunting, and on what little trade they could get. However, with the climatic changes that characterised Europe in these centuries, and which jeopardised agricultural communities all over the continent, their living conditions deteriorated. The Vikings now took to the sea, sometimes to find some honest and peaceful trade, but also to plunder, during the summer months raiding most of the European coastal areas in their well-equipped longboats and returning home with stolen treasure. A silver necklace found in Scandinavia bears an inscription in runic letters which reads: 'We attacked the people of Frisia, and to us came the division of the spoils'. Thus they acquired their reputation as pirates and marauders.

Most of the Vikings who raided the Netherlands hailed from Denmark. They attacked these parts regularly, especially after the death of Charlemagne, as central authority weakened in the Frankish empire due to its repeated division among the many heirs. Texts surviving from these years understandably blame the foreigners for all misery, even though the wars between indigenous princes and nobles caused almost as much damage.

The Vikings concentrated their raids on churches and monasteries – the only source of real riches, with treasure-houses containing gold, silver and precious stones. The population suffered the worst attacks between 879 and 882, when the Vikings set up fortified camps at various places from which they launched their forays. Their leader Godfried the Pirate was even appointed governor of Friesland after consenting to be baptized. He was not alone in conforming. During the first decades of their presence in the South, the Vikings carried out their forays in summer only. Later they also took to spending the winter in the regions they plundered. In an attempt to limit the power of these marauders, land was sometimes granted to their leaders in fee by the Carolingian ruler. In exchange, the Vikings who collaborated were obliged to assist the local ruler in his struggle against other Vikings. Thus, in 841, a Viking called Harald acquired a 'princedom' on the island of Walcheren; a few years later a relation of his called Rorik became ruler over the area which included Dorestad.

Declining prosperity. Departure of the Vikings

As elsewhere in Europe, in the Netherlands, too, most people were totally dependent on agriculture to survive. When nature did not collaborate – which in this period happened increasingly in this region due to the changes of the climate – and when men, instead of working the fields, sowing, harvesting, tending the dikes, et cetera, were forced to go off on a military campaign, the farms were unable to produce what was needed to survive.

When the harvest failed in 892, a severe food shortage was the result. This was the signal for those Vikings who had not yet intermarried with the local population, to withdraw from the Netherlands and to turn their attention to England subsequently; only isolated attacks were made on the Netherlands

The bishops of Utrecht, who had taken refuge elsewhere in the middle of the ninth century, returned to their see in 920.

The last raids of which we have documentary evidence were carried out between 1006 and 1007, when Tiel was one of the places to be plundered. From this time onwards the Vikings were not feared any-more, the more so as most of them had already been converted to Christianity.

Model of the castle at Borssele, in Zeeland. The artificial mound – 'motte' – is crowned by the tower which housed the lord and his family; within the moat is the 'bailey', which contained stables, storerooms and the huts of the servants. This type of castle was normal in the Netherlands from the 11th century onwards (R.M.O. Leiden)

Society and politics after the disintegration of the Carolingian empire: the beginning of regional sovereignty (c. 850-1350)

The development of territorial principalities

The territories that form the provinces of the present-day Netherlands really originated around the year 1000 AD. After the incorporation of the lands of the Frisians, the Saxons and the northern Franks in Lorraine in 855 and in the German Empire in 925, a number of larger principalities was formed by the conquest or merging of smaller counties. Most of these were governed by hereditary counts or dukes. Though they had been little more than regional magnates who had collaborated with central, royal authority in Carolingian times, or had created their own power base precisely by using their office as senior civil servants, they all had gradually acquired both administrative power and extensive lands. Thus, by the tenth and eleventh century, they were largely independent rulers, subject in name only to the German Emperor.

The counts of Holland

The County of Holland was the first to develop. The heart of this region was Kennemara or Kennemerland, which was granted in fee to the Viking Rorik in 862. Another Viking, Gerulf, who was Count of Kennemerland in 885, became the ancestor of the Counts of Holland. A century later one of his descendants, Dirk II, was granted the entire region which he administrated, between the rivers Maas and Vlie, in recognition of his support of the election of Otto II to the office of King of the Romans, i.e. German emperor elect.
Count Dirk III began to levy a toll from the merchant ships sailing in and out of the Maas estuary, laden with profitable trade from both the North Sea and the prosperous heartlands of Europe. A punitive expedition sent against him by the Duke of Lower Lorraine and the Bishop of Utrecht ended in failure as the troops floundered in the sodden marshlands surrounding Vlaardingen. This incident illustrates the independence of the region as a political and administrative entity.

The name *Holland* first appeared in a deed dated 1083, in which Dirk V confirmed the property of the abbey of Egmond and referred to himself as "Count of Holland". The territory of the Counts of Holland was extended considerably in the course of the following two centuries, mainly by conquests over their neighbours. For instance, Flanders was under continual attack for the possession of Zeeland to the east of the Scheldt; this policy eventually met with success. Zeeland to the west of the Scheldt was governed jointly by the dukes of Brabant and the counts Holland; William I is duly referred to in records as Count of Holland and Zeeland.
Holland also waged war on the Frisians, for the possession of West-Friesland. The West-Frisians in their turn regularly raided and plundered Holland as they became isolated from their native country east of the straits connecting the North Sea with the Almere, which grew steadily wider. This part of Friesland did not become subordinate to Holland until 1289, when Count Floris V conquered the region.

Floris V

As young Floris had been only two years old when his father William II died in 1256, a long struggle had ensued for the regency, weakening the authority of the Count for a time. But when Floris came of age and realized the potential of his inheritance, it soon became clear that he was anxious to extend his powers. The Kennemer peasants revolted against the Count in 1274 with the support of Gijsbrecht van Amstel, a nobleman from the Sticht Utrecht who rebelled against Floris's growing power. The dispute was settled in their favour, Floris being obliged to grant the peasants a number of privileges. After this he could do no wrong with them and he was known as "God of the churls". But his relations with the nobles did not improve. Floris sometimes confiscated their possessions to punish them, only returning them in fee in exchange for their oath of fealty. Van Amstel and the lord of Woerden were treated in this way. Some of them took revenge in 1296 by imprisoning Floris in the castle of Muiden. When a group of peasants tried to free him, the nobles murdered him.

The struggle between Floris V and the nobles was a sign of the times. In other principalities too, a landed aristocracy had grown overmighty as the feudal system expanded, and the new magnates increasingly tended to oppose the authority of the ruler. As a result the prince often joined forces with representatives of the towns which were growing in importance economically and consequently politically. As the nobles fought amongst themselves as well, they often appealed for help to the towns, too, which liked to fish in troubled water if there was something to be gained.
The disputes between the 'Hoeksen' (Hooks) and 'Kabeljauwsen' (Cods), two noble factions in the county of Holland, were notorious. They arose over the struggle for succession in the counties of Holland, Zeeland and Hainault, which had formed a personal union since the reign of Floris V. In 1345, the ruling count, William IV, was killed during a campaign to subdue Friesland. In the absence of a son and heir, the Holy Roman Emperor granted the three counties to his own wife Margaretha, sister of the late William. Her son William, still a minor, was appointed as heir.
In the following years however, mother and son disputed each other's right of succession; William had persuaded some of the nobles and a number of towns to take his side in the Kabeljauwse 'party'. The Empress Margaretha formed the Hoeksen 'party' with the support of other nobles. William finally gained possession of Holland and Zeeland in 1354, while Margaretha retained Hainault. At the end of the fourteenth century the feud between 'Hoeksen' and 'Kabeljauwen' flared up once again over a matter of succession. But by then the independence enjoyed by the county was coming to an end; a larger administrative body was beginning to form in north-west Europe as the duchy of Burgundy, originally a possession of France, became independent and by marriage, inheritance and conquest incorporated the principalities of Hainault, Holland and Zeeland.

The diocese of Utrecht

Whereas Holland was a secular principality, the Sticht Utrecht was administered by a religious leader, the bishop. The bishops of Utrecht had been given estates and unused lands by the successive Carolingian kings. From the second half of the tenth century onwards, the Holy Roman emperors also granted them the rights of a count, including his jurisdiction in secular affairs: thus, they were used to govern the empire which, by then, had become too large and was difficult to keep together.
Both in Utrecht and elsewhere in Europe, the episcopal dignity evolved into a position of prime power, coveted by royal relations and members of the aristocracy. For instance, Ansfried, Bishop of Utrecht from 995-1010, had frequently fought at the King's side before his appointment to The Sticht. Only rarely were bishops clerics who really had a spiritual vocation.
In their struggle against the growing power of their vassals, such as the Counts of Holland, the Emperors sought added sup-

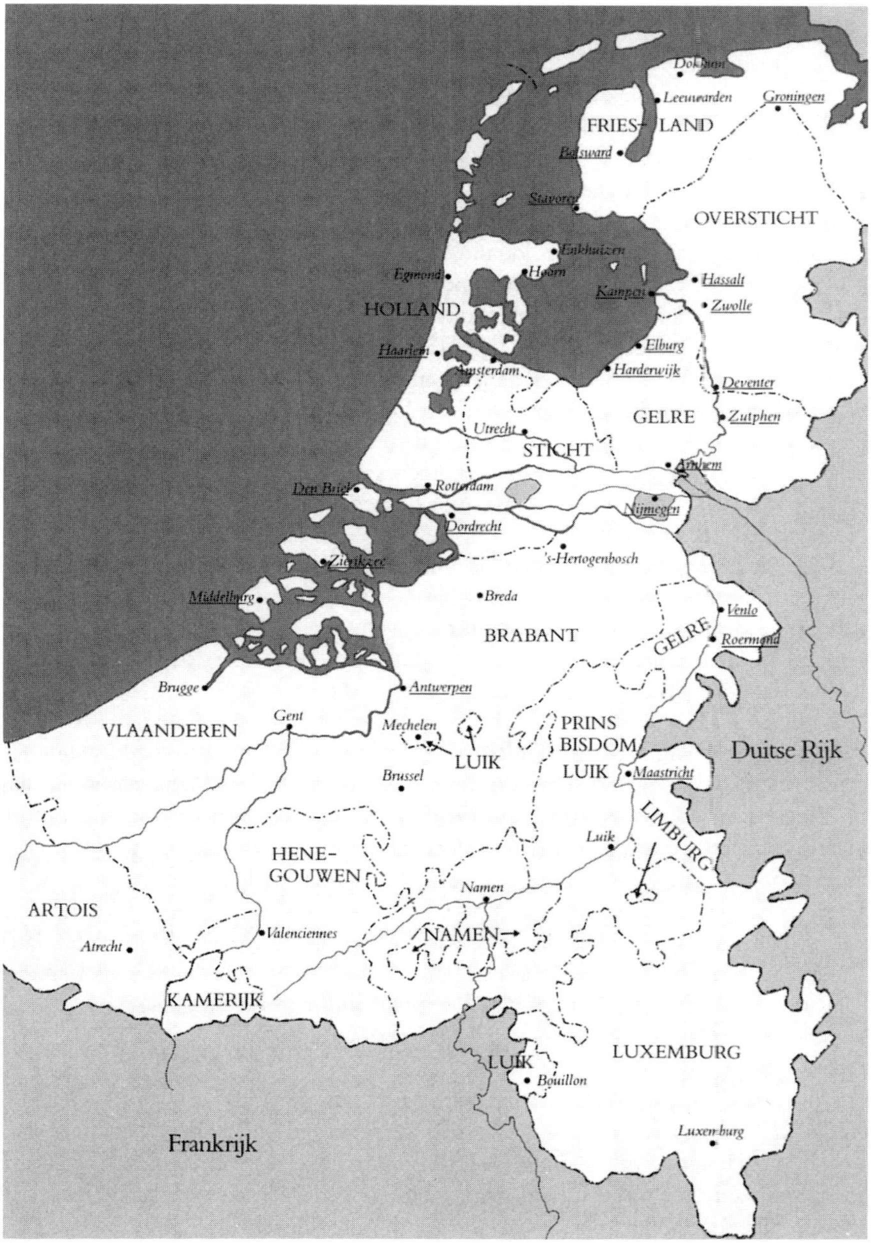

Map of the Netherlands c. 1300

port by giving extensive property to the bishops appointed by them, thus securing their undying loyalty. As the succession to a diocese could never be hereditary, the King was always able to appoint a new bishop who, once more, would be his loyal ally.
In 1024 Bishop Adalbold was presented with the entire county of Drenthe by the German Emperor. In the following years this territory was extended further. The areas in which the bishops wielded secular power were known as 'Lower' Sticht (roughly the Province of Utrecht today) and 'Upper' Sticht (now Overijssel and Drenthe).

In the eleventh century, the so-called Investiture Controversy broke out between the Pope and the Emperor, over the right traditionally claimed by the Emperor to appoint the senior clergy, including the bishops. At the Concordat of Worms in 1122 it was decided that in future, bishops were to be elected by the canons, the high-ranking clergy serving the cathedral of the diocese. In Utrecht they were the canons of the five chapters, led by the dean.
Now that the Emperor had lost his hold on Utrecht, the rulers of small neighbouring states such as Holland and Brabant tried to gain influence over the secular government of The Sticht. When the see of Utrecht became vacant they often advocated the candidacy of their own relations.
Consequently, warlike feuds between parties supporting different candidates frequently rent The Sticht. In 1196 there were two candidates. One was the uncle of the ruling count of Holland, the other a protégé of the Count of Gelderland. In their zeal to acquire the coveted see for their own man, both parties occupied a part of The Sticht. Peace was not restored until a neutral figure was appointed after both contestants had died.
Naturally the inhabitants of both town and country of The Sticht were severely distressed by these military disputes which ravaged the land.
As candidates for the see needed a great amount of money to ensure their election by the canons and to defend their position, they often resorted to pawning their (future) property. In 1331 Bishop Jan van Diest was powerless to intervene when Holland and Gelderland divided The Sticht between them, because he had pledged almost all his possessions as collateral.
Occasionally the bishop was a strong figure, like Jan van Arkel who succeeded in reuniting The Sticht under the episcopal rule in 1362. But even such men were unable to prevent the principality from being drawn into the influence of another increasingly powerful neighbour; eventually Utrecht, like Holland, became part of that greater political entity which was the duchy of Burgundy.

The county, later duchy of Gelderland

The county of Gelderland, which was raised to the rank of a duchy in 1339, was late to develop. It did not begin to resemble the province of Gelderland as it is today until the end of the twelfth century.
Gelderland was not spared the feuds among its aristocracy as already described concerning Holland and Utrecht, in which both nobles and towns fought for greater influence and independence. In Gelderland, too, these feuds often were the result of a dispute over the succession.
In 1343 the families of the Lords of Heeckeren and Bronckhorst interfered with the regency of the heir – a minor – to the first Duke of Gelderland, Reynold II. From 1350 on they also joined in the feud between Reynold III and his brother Edward, until both rivals died in 1371. For many years the 'parties' of the Heeckerens and the Bronckhorsts continued to wage wars, resembling the struggle between the Hoekse and Kabeljauwse groups in Holland.
Like other minor states, Gelderland often waged war on its neighbours. The most powerful of these was the duchy of Brabant.

The duchy of Brabant

Brabant, with its fertile lands and with the wealth brought by the trade of its towns along the Maas and Scheldt rivers, was a major power in north-western Europe. It had considerable influence in the county of Holland during the thirteenth century. Henry II, Duke of Brabant had supported the election of William II, Count of Holland, to be crowned King of the Romans in the German Empire in 1248. William, who was ambitious, tried to use his new position to gain possession of prosperous Flanders. He was prevented from accomplishing this as he was killed during a campaign against the West-Frisians in 1256.
For many years, Brabant also played a leading part in European politics. The Dukes of Brabant were important figures in the German Empire itself, intervening in the struggle between the Staufen and the Welfen, the two parties that contested each other the imperial crown (1198-1214); cleverly, they supported one or the other of these in turn, depending on what they were offered in return. However, this policy brought them into conflict with England or France, which also supported the Welfian and Staufian candidates for the throne respectively.

Brabant had its golden age between 1267 and 1355. Prospects had not been favourable when Henry III died in 1261; a disruptive struggle for the succession, like those in other parts of the Netherlands, seemed inevitable. Henry III's eldest son and heir, another Henry, was mentally and physically handicapped. Henry III's widow succeeded in becoming his regent, permitting co-guardianship to her most influential neighbours, Count Otto II of Gelderland and the Prince-Bishop of Liège. This arrangement, which was made with the support of the clergy, the aristocracy and the towns, gathered in the so-called *States of Brabant*, averted a dynastic crisis and assured peace in the land. When Henry IV came of age he renounced his rights at an assembly of the States, after which he entered a monastery. His younger brother John succeeded him to become one of the most colourful dukes in the history of Brabant.

The 'joyous entry'.

When Duke John III died in 1355 without male issue, he was succeeded by his daughter Joanna. On this occasion a charter was drawn up to specify the rights of the towns. Obviously, the interests of trade and industry, concentrated in the towns, were served by this act, which, however, also indicated the importance of urban economic power for state government, as taxes came increasingly to rely on urban riches; gone had the times wherein the great landed estates, owned by the aristocracy, had been the only sources of wealth; gone, also, had the times wherein the nobles had been the main and often only power in the land.
The act was called the 'Joyous Entry'. It set the seal on a political development in which Brabant led the way for other regions, by defining the relations between the lord and his subjects in a written, sealed statement of the rights and duties of both. For fourteenth-century Brabant it was an occasion of the greatest moment: a contract between the prince and his people.
The 'Joyous Entry' was a guarantee to the towns that the duke would not start a costly war without their permission. It also enabled them to make sure that tax revenues, largely originating in the towns, were spent wisely.

Friesland

Unlike the states described above, Friesland never had a ruling family of its own.
A series of lords from the House of Bruno, from Brunswick, were in power there during the eleventh century. Little is known about them, but their coins, struck in vari-

ous Frisian towns, have been found as far away as Russia.
Actually, Frisia consisted of several small counties such as Staveren – which had already been granted to the Bishop of Utrecht in 1077 – and Oostergo and Westergo, roughly corresponding respectively to the east and west of Friesland as it is today.
When Egbert II, the last of the Bruno's, rebelled against his liege lord, the German Emperor Henry IV, in 1089 Oostergo and Westergo were taken away from him and also granted as a fief to the Bishop of Utrecht, much to the chagrin of Holland. During the twelfth century the bishops of Utrecht and the counts of Holland began to dispute each other the possession of the Frisian counties which were not inclined to obey either ruler. Emperor Frederick Barbarossa eventually decided to allow Utrecht and Holland joint government over Friesland.

In 1197, William, the brother of the ruling count of Holland, was appointed count of Friesland but he did not have long to establish his authority. On the death of his brother in 1203 he also became count of Holland. In the absence of their lord, the Frisians no longer felt accountable to him. They were free once more. Feuds now broke out between several great landowning families who attacked each other from their strongholds with small armies. This strife, comparable to that in other principalities, was made worse by the influence of the mighty monasteries of the Cistercian and Norbertine orders. The majority of monks in Frisian monasteries during the thirteenth century were lay brothers who had not taken vows. They sometimes grew overmighty in which case monastic discipline slackened or even disappeared. In about 1340 a feud broke out between the monasteries of Bloemkamp and Lidlum. Bloemkamp was a Cistercian monastery. As the monks belonging to this order wore grey habits, they were called grey – 'schier' – friars or 'Schieringers'. This accounts for the name of the island Schiermonnikoog which belonged to the monastery at that time. The monks of Lidlum belonged to the Norbertine order. Because their wealth was mainly based on cattle, they were known as 'Vetkopers' (butter-boxes). Therefore Frisian party-feuds were called after the struggle between the 'Schieringers' and the 'Vetkopers'.

This struggle flared up continually during the second half of the fourteenth and the entire fifteenth century, when peasants and burghers, clergy and laymen and the various noble families all fought among themselves. The Schieringers, who dominated in Oostergo were usually in favour of Frisian independence; the Vetkopers, who lived mainly in what is now the Province of Friesland, were inclined to join forces with Holland. These feuds led to plundering, raiding and arson, causing great harm to the Frisian people in the absence of a higher authority to control them.
Occasionally one of the counts of Holland attempted to claim the rights of Holland to Friesland, still valid in name.
In 1345, William IV raised a large army in order to subdue the Frisians. He was killed and his army was defeated soundly during the ensuing Battle of Warns, a village in the southwest of Friesland.
Later attempts to re-establish the authority of the counts over Friesland, undertaken at the end of the fourteenth century also met with failure. However, the Frisians finally lost their freedom at the end of the fifteenth century, and then not to the counts of Holland but to the descendant of the Burgundian dukes, who had now become German Emperor. He subjected rebellious Friesland to his own direct rule by appointing a 'Stadhouder' or Lieutenant.

The great tower of Utrecht cathedral. Building started in 1321 and was finished in 1382. It is shown here in a 19th-century coloured lithograph

Economy and politics since c. 1000: the beginnings of an urban economy

Construction of dykes and reclamation of land

After the turn of the millennium, with the Vikings ceasing their raids, the climate getting milder and, consequently, conditions for regular agrarian production improving, the population began to increase. Also, the political situation stabilized, creating peace and order. To meet the need for more land by the people who still lived mainly by agriculture and cattle farming, wasteland now was increasingly cultivated. Also, low-lying areas were drained and protected by dykes, and marshland was reclaimed. The farmers of Holland and Friesland became so skilled at this work that, in 1113, the Archbishop of Hamburg offered them land in Saxony for reclamation. In this way they helped to colonize and populate eastern Germany.

In addition to the need for more land, the rising sea level – caused by the gradual melting of the polarice – also necessitated the construction of dykes. In the thirteenth century seawater poured into the Netherlands via the Almere. The construction of sea dykes, such as the dyke between Harlingen and Stavoren, in Friesland, became a dire necessity to save the country from regular inundation and siltation.

Organizations called water boards were now formed to ensure that the dykes were kept in good repair and to regulate the water level in low-lying areas. This was one example of a general tendency to order and regulate everyday life.
The same tendency was also noticeable in the Church, where episcopal re-organization took place in the dioceses involving the appointment of archdeacons and suffragan bishops. At a lower level, large parishes were split up into numerous smaller ones, with boundaries corresponding roughly to those of a village in order to increase the hold on Churchlife and the community.

The economy and the monasteries

The first monasteries in this country were often established by the richest and most powerful people, the regional princes and the nobles. For instance, Rijnsburg Abbey was founded by Countess Petronella of Holland in 1133.
The monasteries were large communities with sometimes as many as a thousand inmates. Most of them were in the countryside, and their main activities besides their spiritual life was the management of their often extensive estates; they instigated a great deal of useful work, for the monks were foremost in constructing dykes and pioneers in reclaiming land and cultivating wasteland.
In the fourteenth century, smaller monasteries arose, usually with a more contemplative background. They were not situated in the rural areas, but in the towns which had been founded during the preceding centuries. There, the growing population felt the need for spiritual care, but also for the kind of education that, up till then, only monks and nuns were able to provide.

The rise of the towns

The resurgence of old towns, dating from the Roman period, as well as the rise of new towns in the eleventh and twelfth centuries, though partly due to the growing population, was also influenced by the slow but steady increase in trade and industry. The food situation improved with higher production through higher yield ratios and better transport of grain and other foodstuffs; people now even could afford to specialize, both in agriculture and in industry, and

make a better profit by producing for the interregional market.
During the eleventh and twelfth centuries Europe renewed and stepped up its commercial contacts with important overseas regions. Trade with the Near East, so rich in luxury goods from all over farther Asia, was resumed after the first crusade in 1096. England, which was able to produce huge quantities of wool for the textile industry, was enmeshed in a continental trade network after the duke of Normandy had conquered it in 1066.
Trade and industry were concentrated in the towns, which also drew produce from the surrounding rural areas at the weekly markets and annual fairs. Supplies of wood and other primary provisions had to be brought into these trading centres for the daily needs of the townspeople who could not produce these for themselves.

New waterways

As trade increased, and the range of products grew in number and volume, larger ships were needed which, however, could not navigate the old inland waterways. Other trade routes came into use, including one over the North Sea through the Sound into the Baltic Sea. This meant that new markets came within reach, such as the rich Baltic ports, where there was a plentiful supply of grain and wood for shipment to the Netherlands. This, specifically, enabled those who were economically adventurous to start specializing in industry rather than continuing to work in agriculture for their own direct need.
Now, the old trading centres of Tiel and Utrecht, which depended on the great rivers to transport their merchandise, could no longer compete with the seaports in the north such as Stavoren, Leeuwarden, Groningen, Dokkum and Bolsward. From these ports merchant ships set out for Germany, England and the Scottish kingdom.

The 'Kampervoort', relic of the past wealth and power of the Hansa town of Kampen

The Hansa towns

Merchants also navigated the Sound from towns on the Zuider Zee and the River IJssel, including Harderwijk, Elburg, Deventer and Kampen; this was known as 'around-country shipping' – Ommelandvaart. Many of these towns joined the Hanseatic League, probably the first truly international trade organization, ever: a merchant guild which united numerous German and Dutch trading towns to defend their joint interests.
The independent position taken by these towns in economic affairs was partly due to the freedom enjoyed by town councils in decision making. This was one of the privileges laid down in the town charter, granted by the various princes ruling in this region to the towns in their territory. In return they hoped for financial support in their wars, from the ever richer and more powerful merchants. One of the earliest examples of a charter of this kind dates from 1185, when Duke Henry I of Brabant granted a number of privileges to 's Hertogenbosch. Later charters in the Dutch regions often followed the pattern set in this early example. Thus, the privileges granted to Haarlem and 's Gravenzande in 1245 by Count William II of Holland were based on those of "Den Bosch".

The political power of the towns

The wealth and the relative political and institutional independence afforded by their privileges enabled the towns to assume political power alongside the other power groups, the ruler and his bureaucracy, the aristocracy and the Church. By the fifteenth century many of the towns operated as virtually independent communities, also forming strong and sometimes decisive political factions in the many party feuds dividing the various states. They often intervened in questions of succession as they knew by experience how damaging the resulting wars could be: they cost money and hampered trade. No longer did town councils unquestioningly submit to taxation or the obligation to take part in a war; like the aristocracy, they wanted to be consulted first by the central government. In most principalities, this led to the increasingly regular convening of consultative meetings between representatives of the leading clergy, the aristocracy and the representatives of the towns, which came to be known as the Assembly of the Estates. The first of these more or less regular meetings was convened in Brabant, in 1312, when Duke John II, forced to ensure the co-operation of his mighty subjects, issued the so-called Charter of Kortenberg, calling for a council of fourteen members to be formed, comprising four members of the aristocracy, and ten representatives from the towns.
The right of this council to be consulted on certain matters of state mentioned above was later confirmed in the 'Joyous Entry'. United in a personal union under Count William V, the joint Estates of the counties of Holland, Zeeland and Hainault drew up new regulations in 1362 to give themselves considerable political influence.
In the Sticht, the burghers of the city of Utrecht already had acquired a say in the election of a new bishop in the twelfth century. Finally, the right to assemble of the Estates, in which the towns and the aristocracy (each representing its own 'estate') formed a union, was founded on the 'Charter for the Land' issued in 1375 by Bishop Arnold of Horn, who had been obliged to make concessions after the unfortunate outcome of a war against Holland and Gelderland.
In Gelre, too, fear that the question of succession would stir up trouble, prompted the aristocracy and the towns to join forces and convince the duke that he would do better to seek the co-operation of the political-economic elite of his duchy before taking major decisions. Duke Reynold IV acknow-

ledged the rights of the 'States of Gelderland' in 1419.
Thus, in most early Dutch states, some form of consensual government, however oligarchic, was growing by the fourteenth century.

The church of St. Gervase, Maastricht as it is today

Reliquary of St. Gervase. One of the finest examples of 12th-century silversmith's work in the 'Maasland-Romanesque' style

Culture: the role of the urban bourgeoisie

The rise of the towns also had other effects. Till the eleventh century, cultural activity as far as it has left any traces was mainly confined to the aristocracy and the clergy. Particularly in the monasteries, the surviving Greek and Latin classics were preserved and copied, and the first chronicles recording contemporary life were written, here, by such monks as Emo and Menko in the thirteenth century. Both Emo and Menko later became abbot of the Bloemhof monastery in Groningen.
Latin was the language used for writing in the monasteries, from the thirteenth century onwards. The result of the rise of towns and the growing wealth of the burghers was that a form of Dutch vernacular was used increasingly in urban writing. The 'Verse Chronicle' of Melis Stoke – dating from soon after 1300 – and the works of Jacob van Maerlant are good examples of a new, urban culture.

As far as these ages have left any architectural remains at all, they tend to be specimens of ecclesiastical architecture. The Romanesque style, particularly in the north, was mainly the art of the rural areas: buildings with massive walls, windows and doors with rounded arches and the simple saddle-roof towers. Examples of this Romanesque architecture can still be found today in the villages of the northern provinces of Groningen en Friesland.
The surviving Romanesque architecture in the south of the country, represented by the lovely churches of St. Gervase and of Our Lady in Maastricht, is more monumental and belongs to another stream known as the Maasland style. Famed, too, for its wrought-iron work, this style reached its peak in the eleventh and twelfth centuries. Magnificent reliquaries were made here. Perhaps the loveliest of these is the shrine of St. Gervase which is still kept in the church devoted to him.
There were craftsmen working in iron, silver and gold in the North, too, but they did not achieve the high standard of the south. What is left of their work consists mainly of coins and monastic seals, including that of Egmond Abbey. The oldest surviving shrine from the North was made in Utrecht in 1362.

Part of the big 'view of Amersfoort' painted by Matthias Withoos in 1671. It shows the church of Our Lady and its tower, from the north-west

A lighter and more elegant architecture, later called Gothic, developed in the towns during the fourteenth and fifteenth centuries, to create ever lovelier churches with tall spires and stained-glass windows.
The most famous fourteenth-century gothic buildings in this country can be seen in Utrecht and 's Hertogenbosch. Building on the tower of the Dom-church in Utrecht began in 1321, despite the voices of those who criticised it as a sign of arrogance and a form of despicable waste. It was designed by a master builder, who, unlike most of his colleagues during these ages, is known to us by his name, Jan van Henegouwen; it was completed in 1382, 110 metres in height. The choir of this church also dates from the fourteenth century. The magnificent cathedral of St. John in 's Hertogenbosch was built in the same period.
The best-known example of a secular gothic building is the 'Ridderzaal' or Knights' Hall in The Hague, which was built at the end of the thirteenth century by order of Count Floris V of Holland. This hall, which has been rather overrestored in the 19th century, is the scene of the annual ceremony of the opening of Parliament.

The fine arts

Painting does not seem to have flourished in the Netherlands until the fourteenth century. There was some miniature painting, usually illustrations to the manuscripts written in the monasteries. This form of art, in contrast with others, was but little influenced by awakening cultural activity in the towns. Its surviving examples are found in missals made for nobles and clergy, particularly in Utrecht and Gelderland.
Monumental painting before 1350 was rare and is represented only by a few murals. There are also a few late fourteenth-century painted panels most of which were made in Gelderland and Utrecht, too. They were memorial tableaux, to be placed in churches near the tomb of the high-ranking person to whom they were dedicated.
Sculpture from this period is also scarce. The few remaining works are mainly monuments to nobles and high-ranking clergy, such as the tomb of Jan van Arkel in the great church at Gorinchem.
In the fifteenth century, with wealth increasing in Holland, Zeeland and Utrecht through profits made both in agriculture and in trade and industry, the affluent citizens became interested in showing their material and also political power, as well as in adorning their homes and towns.
Portraits were now widely produced – documenting the continuity of patrician families, and showing the visitor an impressive public 'face' – but landscapes, too, became increasingly popular.

Religion in the towns

In general, all culture in this period silently but evocatively reflects the essential part played by religion in everyday life. Until the fourteenth century the aristocracy and the clergy still were the leading patrons of the arts; but the class of wealthy burghers which had developed in the towns was gradually coming into its own. It is significant that in religion too, it was this new class which showed itself to be susceptible to new trends.
The establishment of small monasteries in the towns, besides the big ones that continued to flourish in the countryside, was mentioned above. Many of these had their roots in the Modern Devotion, a movement started by Geert Grote of Deventer c. 1384. Its object was to try and get as broad as possible a range of people to return to a simple way of life based on religion. Education was to be its instrument, but that meant that it had to be provided to other than elite children, only. Strangely, these ideas appealed predominantly to the reasonably educated and wealthy citizens who now formed religious brotherhoods, but without the obligation to take vows. These religious congregations later often joined one of the existing monastic orders, usually the Franciscans, famous for their poverty and piety.

Society and politics in the Burgundian-Hapsburg Empire. Centralization of power and authority (1350-1550)

The period from the tenth to the fourteenth century saw the foundation and growth of regional states in the Netherlands, later to become the provinces of the present kingdom. One might argue that an important part of the character of the Netherlands was formed during this time, both in its geographic and economic, and its political and cultural aspects. Towards the end of this period we see the towns taking their place beside the ruler, the aristocracy and the clergy, increasingly influencing economic and political life. Society in the Netherlands gradually became more urban and the culture of the affluent burghers set the tone.

The situation from 1350 onwards

About 1350 most of the future regions of the Netherlands were already established as independent states, only nominally under the suzerainty of the Holy Roman Emperor. Yet, by the same time, the authority of the various dynasties had gradually dwindled due to internal conflicts and the rise of the burghers; the resulting assemblies of the Estates imposed all kinds of limits on the rulers, mainly to curb expenditure. In the fifteenth century there were two contrasting developments. On the one hand many towns grew into robust little states going their own way; on the other hand the power over the various principalities became concentrated in one single family, that of the Dukes of Burgundy alone, who acquired it through marriages, inheritance and wars.

Philip the Bold (1342-1404) and his matrimonial policy

In 1363 the then King of France gave the French Duchy of Burgundy to his son Philip, surnamed the Bold, who married Margaretha of Flanders, the heiress to the independent County of Burgundy (Franche-Comté) in 1369. On the death of his father-in-law in 1384 Philip also inherited the states of Flanders, Artois, Nevers and Rethel, as well as two important towns won from Brabant – Antwerp and Mechlin. From then on, the Burgundian dukes operated largely independently from, and most often in opposition to the kingdom of France. Although they lost some ground in the south, they successfully continued to extend their power northwards.
Philip succeeded in arranging favourable marriages for his children. A double wedding took place in 1385, the first between his son John, later known as John the Fearless, and Margaretha of Bavaria; the second between his daughter Margaretha and the brother of Margaretha of Bavaria, William VI, who became Count of Holland, Zeeland and Hainault in 1404. As the latter had no son, he was succeeded on his death in 1417 by his daughter Jacqueline of Bavaria who was married to Duke John IV of Brabant. Inevitably, problems brewed between Burgundy and Holland-Brabant.

Philip the Good (1396-1467)

It was Philip the Good, son of John the Fearless, who succeeded in uniting all these regions under his rule. He engaged in a fierce struggle with his cousin Jacqueline of Bavaria, who, in successive marriages, had born no children to succeed her; during these feuds, the disputes between the Hoekses and Kabeljauwses flared up again as bitterly as ever. Finally, a compromise was reached in 1428. This entailed that Jacqueline relinquished her real power to Philip, while keeping her titles. Neither was she free to remarry without the permission of Philip, of her mother, who played a rather devious role, and the assembled

17th-century engraving showing Philip the Good (1396-1467), Duke of Burgundy, Count of Holland, Zeeland and Hainault; he also inherited Brabant and Luxembourg

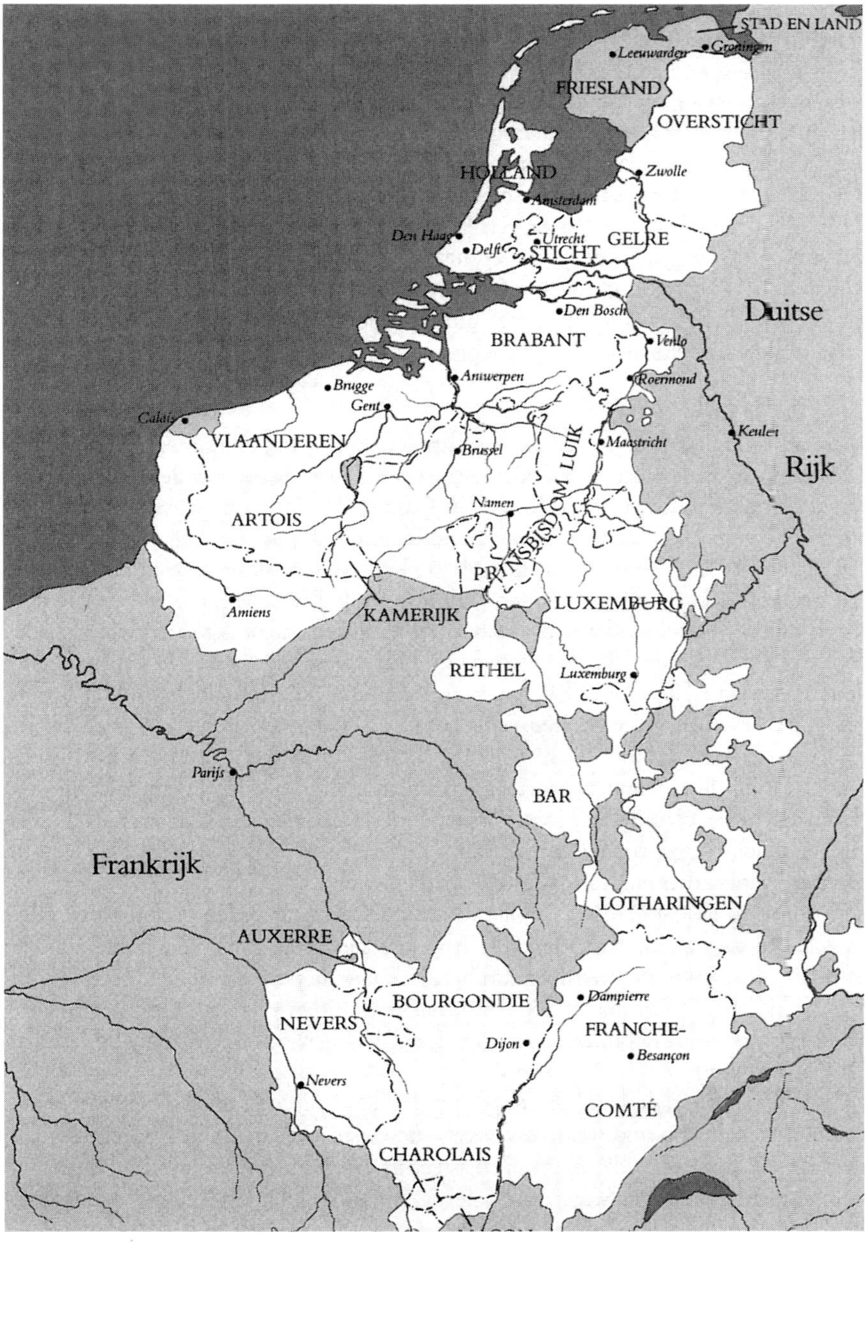

Map of the Burgundian Netherlands at the death of Charles the Bold

Estates of her regions. When, in spite of this treaty, Jacqueline secretly married the Zeeland noble Frank van Borselen, she also forfeited her titles and Philip succeeded her as Count of Holland, Zeeland and Hainault.

Brabant had already come into Philip's possession in 1430 because his two ducal cousins had died childless. In 1451 he also inherited Luxembourg with the result that, in addition to the ancestral part of Burgundy, his empire then included the present territory of Belgium, Luxembourg and a large chunk of the Netherlands. Gelderland, Utrecht, Friesland and Groningen were not yet a part of it. But in 1456 Utrecht, and with it Overijssel and Drenthe were brought into the Burgundian camp when Philip succeeded in having his bastard son David appointed bishop. Friesland stayed out of Burgundian reach for a long time. Groningen too, held on to its independence for the time being with occasional support from the Dukes of Gelderland who came to look upon the encroaching Burgundians as their arch enemies, and, consequently, became the toughest opponents of Burgundian expansion.

Charles the Bold (1433-1477)

Like his father before him, Charles the Bold, son and heir of Philip the Good, came into conflict with Gelderland. He had high hopes for his empire, seeking to expand it to equal the size of the former Carolingian central empire of Lothair in the ninth century and hoping to seal his triumphs by gaining the title of king from the Holy Roman Emperor.

Forced to deftly manoeuvre in international politics, Charles formed an alliance with the English. The English king, himself an enemy of France, was willing to support the Burgundians in their struggle against France, which grew uneasier as Burgundy grew more powerful. In another move, Charles annexed Gelderland to the Burgundian empire in 1473. He conquered Lorraine in the same year so that his many states in the Netherlands now adjoined his Burgundian lands. But in 1476 the people of Lorraine rebelled. In 1477 the duke was killed in an attempt to regain the capital, Nancy. He was succeeded by his only child, his daughter Mary, who had been promised to the Emperor's son. When she married Maximilian I of Habsburg, Archduke of Austria, of the family which had produced German emperors for many decades, the Burgundian and Habsburg empires were united.

Meanwhile, the Hoeksen-party in Holland continued to oppose Burgundy, attempting to undermine Burgundian authority as best it could. However, the rebels were driven over the border to the city of Utrecht from where, between 1481 and 1483, they carried on a bitter struggle against Bishop David of Burgundy and Emperor Maximilian of Habsburg, husband of Mary of Burgundy and, in her lieu, the acting new count of Holland.
Mary died in 1482, and Maximilian obtained the regency for their son and heir Philip, later known as Philip the Fair.
The Hoeksen were defeated at Utrecht in 1483. However, in 1488 they returned to the field against the Burgundians and even succeeded in taking the city of Rotterdam, only to be defeated again two years later.
Meanwhile Gelderland was more successful in freeing itself from Burgundian bondage. Philip the Fair, who came of age in 1493, did not at first take kindly to the idea of subjecting Gelderland once again. But on the insistence of his father Maximilian, he conquered the duchy in 1504. Charles, Duke of Gelderland then formed an alliance with the French king. He attempted to regain his lands by means of raids headed by the dreaded military commander Maarten van Rossum. With the help of, among others, the Frisian pirate "Grote Pier", he also succeed-

ed in subduing Groningen and Friesland for a time. Groningen then acknowledged him as its overlord.

Burgundy, Hapsburg and the world: Philip the Fair (1478-1506)

Surveying the titles of Philip the Fair, it was obvious how mighty Burgundy had become. Not only was he Duke of Burgundy, he also was count or duke of more than a dozen states in the Netherlands regions. As his father's son he was also Archduke of Austria. His potential power greatly increased when, in 1495, he married Joanna of Castile, the only remaining successor to her mother's kingdom of Castile and her father's kingdom of Aragon. These regions were to form the heart of Spain as it is today. On the death of his mother-in-law in 1506 Philip also became King of Castile, and, with it, of Castile's recently acquired American possessions. He died in the same year.

The Netherlands as part of an international union: Emperor Charles V (1500-1558)

Because of the marriage of Philip the Fair and Joanna of Castile and Aragon, their eldest son Charles was destined to inherit an empire that already was beginning to span the world. He was born in Ghent in 1500 and brought up in the humanist tradi-

Tomb of Charles the Bold in the church of Our Lady at Bruges

tion by the scholar Adrian Boeyens; through Charles' influence, Adrian later was made a cardinal and, eventually, was chosen pope. Thus, Hadrian VI became the first Dutch successor of St. Peter, not much loved in Italy because of his stern policy against the Church's decadence – he was the last non-Italian pope till the end of the twentieth century.
On the death of his father in 1506, Charles came into the entire Burgundian inheritance, including the many duchies and counties that together were now being called the Netherlands for the first time. He was declared of age in 1515, and in 1516, on the death of his grandfather Ferdinand who had governed Castile as Regent since 1506, he became king of both the Spanish kingdoms, Aragon – with Naples-Sicily and the Duchy of Milan – and Castile, which also included Granada, conquered in 1492, and the Castilian claims on the New World established after Columbus' voyages in 1492: Mexico, which was conquered in 1519 by Spanish adventurers; Peru, taken from the Inca's in 1532, and the Philippine islands, acquired in the same decades.
He also inherited the Austrian States on the death of his grandfather Maximilian in 1519. Finally, by dint of much intrigue and bribery he became Emperor of the Holy Roman Empire.

Charles V (1500-1558), Lord of the Netherlands, Emperor of the German Empire, King of Spain, etc. Over his empire 'the sun never set'

All the regions of this empire remained separate administrative entities. Meanwhile, Burgundy itself had been regained by France, but Gelderland, Groningen, Friesland and The Sticht had been added to the Burgundian empire when Gelderland at last surrendered to Charles V, accepting the Treaty of Venlo in 1543. Groningen had already acknowledged him as overlord in 1536, and in The Sticht too he had acquired the secular power with the approval of his former tutor, Pope Hadrian.
To govern his many states in North-western Europe, now together known as the 'Seventeen United Netherlands', Charles, accepting that he could not rule them in person, appointed a royal governor, to be stationed in Brussels. The first to fill this hugely important position – for Charles knew that much of his wealth came from these unruly regions – was his aunt Margaretha, dowager-duchess of Savoy, as he preferred to choose trustworthy relatives; she was followed by his sister, Mary, queen-dowager of Hungary. He himself only occasionally visited the Netherlands. He spent most of his time fighting his enemies:

France, which, understandably, opposed the Habsburgs who now were encircling it; the princes of the German Empire, who resented an emperor who yielded real power, and the Protestants in the German states; and, of course, the armies of the Islamic Turks, advancing on the Balkans and across the Mediterranean.

The Netherlands' regions and the cities oppose the Hapsburg policy of centralization

From the late fifteenth century onwards, the regional representative assemblies, the Estates, composed of the clergy, the aristocracy and the towns, developed into the strongest opponents of the central authority which the Burgundians and Habsburgs were trying to establish. Though they ruled each of these regions separately – as duke, count or lord – the Burgundian Habsburgs felt that a common policy and administration for all the Netherlands was necessary, if only to improve their income from these states' fiscal resources, which they needed to wage the wars caused by their wish to safeguard their enormous empire; to them, scrupulously respecting regional privileges and maintaining the individuality of each state was less than efficient, administratively and politically. In every region, they set up a well-oiled civil service headed by a chancellor. In addition there was an advisory body, a council of high-ranking nobles, professional administrators and lawyers. They established chambers of accounts and courts of justice in the various regions; these were finally centralized by Charles the Bold under a General Chamber of Accounts for all his regions and a Supreme Court known as the Parliament of Mechlin.

To counteract the Burgundian efforts towards centralization, a number of towns and cities took action. For instance, Utrecht and Amersfoort played an important part in the Hoeksen and Kabeljauwsen feuds between 1481 and 1483. Both cities had already denied the episcopal judges jurisdiction in case of capital crimes committed within their walls. They also decided to elect their own town council which then drew up their own statutes and even went so far as to appoint the bailiff, traditionally the local personification of princely power. Undeniably, however, in the sixteenth century the further development of central, Habsburg government in the various regions managed to curb the independence of the cities, but the burghers continued to influence the administration through their participation in the regional assemblies or 'States'.

The States-General and the Grand Council

However, the regional assemblies, too, were affected by centralization. In 1464, they convened for the first time together, at Bruges, to decide whether Duke Philip the Good should be enabled to go on a crusade. They were called the "States-General" and soon became a permanent feature in the government of the Burgundian lands when their role was inscribed in the "Grand Privilege" issued by Mary of Burgundy in 1477, when she succeeded her father and wanted her Habsburg husband acknowledged as ruler of all her states. The States-General demanded that from now one they would be allowed to meet if it pleased them, and that the ruler would never start a war without their consent. Also, the Parliament of Mechlin and the General Chamber of Accounts – hated instruments of central rule – were disbanded and a Grand Council was formed with 25 members and a chancellor to assist the duchess in her government. The rulers did not fail to retaliate and, in 1504, the Parliament of Mechlin was reinstated as a Supreme Court, but the States-General retained its powers. Charles V, trying to make the Grand Council into an instrument of his own, divided it into a Council of Finances, a Privy Council and the Council of State.

Engraving showing the moment – October 25, 1555 – when Charles V transferred his power over the seventeen Netherlands to his son Philip (Mary of Hungary and Cardinal Granvelle flank the throne)

The last, meant to be a general advisory council, consisted of leading civil servants and the first nobles of the Netherlands. But the Emperor's governors who ruled in Brussels, mostly consulted with the civil servants, the instruments of central power.

The economy: the growing importance of the towns of Holland

After 1350, the population of Europe had fallen drastically as a result of a small 'ice age', during which a series of failed harvests led to famine and weakness. Hundreds of thousands of people fell prey to the great plague epidemics. The resulting economic depression lasted into the fifteenth century, when the first signs of recovery appeared. Grain was needed in the whole of Western Europe, and there was a rich supply of it in the Baltic countries and in Central Europe.

Precisely through its traditional trading connections, the region of Holland was now growing in importance in the Netherlands. From the fourteenth century, Dordrecht already had been playing a leading part in trading via the great rivers, having acquired the staple right for all traffic on the river Rhine in 1344; it soon became a central market, or 'staple town.
After 1400, other towns of Holland began to join in international trading, especially to the Baltic, at the expense of the old Hansa towns. Most towns in Holland had never joined the Hanseatic League, and consequently could not be bothered with its rules. Amsterdam became the most serious rival, but Hoorn and Enkhuizen also prospered. The importance, but also the vulnerability of trade to the Baltic was revealed by the famine which struck the Netherlands when the passage through the Sound was closed between 1531 and 1537, as a result of a war of succession in Denmark. The time that people in Holland were able to live on the produce of their own land having been long past, the Dutch had to rely on large stores of grain, or increase the agricultural surface to accommodate more mouths.
Of course, problems were less acute in the mostly agricultural inland states, which, moreover, were less densely populated.
Fishing at sea had became increasingly important to the towns of Holland too. The discovery, at the end of the fourteenth century, of the curing of herring, which enabled the fishermen to salt and preserve it aboard, led to a boom in herring-fishing. As a result of this, the shipbuilding industry flourished once more.
Existing industries continued to grow after 1400. Leiden and Haarlem became the leading centres in the manufacture of cloth from English wool. Beer was brewed in large quantities at Delft, Gouda, Haarlem and Amersfoort, some of it for export.
Holland's rural areas were at a disadvantage in this economic development of the towns. The latter were important to the Count – now the Duke of Burgundy and later Charles V – in view of the tax revenues. For this reason some forms of industry were forbidden in the countryside in order to protect their interests in the towns. Inevitably this led to urbanization. Also, in some of the larger towns a fairly extensive proletariat became noticeable.

By 1500, among the regions of the northern Netherlands, Holland had taken the lead in the economy; this was to have its effect on politics in the centuries which followed.

Mural depicting Christ crucified, found in the 14th-century catacombes of the Franciscan monastery at Dordrecht (R.M.O. Leiden)

Culture (1300-1550): the emergence of new trends

Renaissance and humanism

Between 1300 and 1550, all over Europe changes took place in – mostly – elite culture, which deeply influenced the way European man looked at himself and at his world. Gradually, educated people, the reading public, began to ask what was the status of the knowledge sanctioned by and transmitted through the agencies of the Church; especially man's relationship to God and to the cosmos, God's creation, was now studied from a more empirical point of view; both texts and the 'book of nature' served as sources to be critically perused, to enable man to form his own opinions, and thus fulfil his duty to be really human.
In the Netherlands, this Humanism found its greatest champion in Desiderius Erasmus of Rotterdam (1469-1536). This scholar, already famous in his own day, applied the Humanist principle of studying the classics in their original text to Christianity. Thus, he published the first scholarly edition of the Greek version of the New Testament.
His views on ethics and religion were akin to the spirit of the Modern Devotion. He believed in tolerance and peace, advocating a pure and sober form of religion – but within the context of the Roman Catholic Church, despite his own and others'growing criticism of its practices.

The Renaissance is traditionally linked to Humanism, of which it is the more visible expression, showing itself in new forms of architecture, sculpture any painting, inspired by the discovery of the art of the ancient Romans and Greeks. Originating in Italy, the Renaissance, too, spread to the North, although, there, architecture long retained its earlier, gothic forms.

Education and literature

Many Dutch humanists were able to propound their ideas widely because they taught at the Latin schools. These schools gradually became the leading educational institutions in the Netherlands. They were originally attached to the parish churches for the specific purpose of training the prospective clergy. As the burghers grew more affluent they too began to show an interest in education. Town councils often took it upon themselves to govern these schools. In the sixteenth century the council schools were sometimes eclipsed by private schools. The authorities reacted by imposing fines, or by banning some subjects from the curriculum. Girls were sometimes admitted to these private schools but not to council schools. Meanwhile, in the Netherlands the provision of education for both the rich and the poor had become far greater than in most other European countries. The comparatively low percentage of illiterate people in this country never failed to astonish contemporaries in the sixteenth century.
The invention of printing in the middle of the fifteenth century started a real cultural revolution, as it increased opportunities for people to buy and read books for themselves. Both education and printing induced cultural development in larger groups of the population. The well-to-do burghers took up literature, which had always been the domain of the aristocracy. Merchants, bankers and entrepreneurs formed 'chambers of rhetoric' where they studied poetry, but they also endeavoured to standardize Dutch spelling. There was a shift from chivalrous poetry towards dramatic art during the sixteenth century, when both playwriting and the performance of plays with a clear moral message became popular.

A representation of St. Anna, her daughter the Virgin Mary, and Jesus, carved in oak, beginning of the 16th century (Museum Catharijneconvent, Utrecht)

Architecture, sculpture and painting

Wealthy townspeople also began to take an active interest in architecture. They frequently built their houses of stone in the new Gothic style, and they often contributed generously to the building of churches and town halls. Towns such as Amersfoort, Rhenen, Delft and Breda vied proudly with each other by means of their steeples, sometimes over a 100 metres tall, which often adjoined the parish church. They demonstrate how closely religion, culture and politics were intertwined at that time.
Before 1550 sculpture was usually inspired and commissioned by the aristocracy and the clergy. But the burghers, too, began to subscribe to religious art as they joined fraternities; they built special fraternity chapels, or at the least they maintained an altar in the parish church. The most famous fifteenth-century sculptor was Adriaen van Wesel of Utrecht (c.1420-1500), who created an altar to the Virgin Mary in St.James's church at 's Hertogenbosch for the Illustrious Fraternity of Our Lady.

Together with a few of its smaller neighbouring towns, Utrecht had been the cultural heart of the Netherlands since about 1400. Both the episcopacy and the often aristocratic canons of the five chapters employed numerous skilled artists. Miniature painting blossomed here in the first half of the fifteenth century. The Book of Hours made c. 1430 for Catherine of Cleves, wife of Duke Arnold of Gelderland, is the best-known example of this art. The miniature painting of Utrecht distinguished itself from that of the Southern Netherlands by its realism and the choice of subjects from everyday life, characteristics which prevailed in Dutch art for centuries.
Dutch painting, which hardly existed before 1400, first appeared near Utrecht, too, in Gouda, Oudewater and Schoonhoven. The earliest known Dutch portrait, portraying

the Lady Lijsbeth van Duvenvoirde, was painted on parchment in 1430.
The flourishing cities and towns of Holland also stimulated the art of painting in the second half of the fifteenth century. The cultural centre transferred to Haarlem where several artists from Utrecht set up their easels, including Albert van Ouwater. Well-known members of the Haarlem school of artists were Geertgen tot Sint Jans (c. 1467-1495) and Dierik Bouts (c. 1475), who later moved on to Louvain.
During the first half of the sixteenth century, the renaissance style made rapid headway in painting and sculpture. This was mainly the result of the many journeys to Italy undertaken by artists from this time onwards. The first artist known to have made the trip was Jan Gossaert, who also worked at the court of Bishop David of Burgundy. His pupil Jan van Scorel (1495-1562), well-known for his portraits and religious works, followed his example. Lucas van Leyden (1494-1533) was famous in his own day for his portraits and altarpieces, and especially for his engravings. This form of art was in great demand by the wealthy burghers, partly because woodcuts were cheaper than oil paintings.
The artist Hieronymus Bosch (1450-1516) worked in Brabant, principally at 's Hertogenbosch. Some people maintain that the spirit of the middle ages still shows strong in his somewhat visionary work, inspired perhaps by the misery of contemporary rural life and the persecution of witchcraft just now beginning.
This may be true, for while new age was awakening, the earlier cultures lingered on.

Illuminated breviary – prayer book – made for Beatrix of Assendelft, Delft c. 1485 (Museum Catharijneconvent, Utrecht)

Luther and Calvin

In religion, enthusiasm for the sober approach preached by the Modern Devotion at the end of the fourteenth century had completely waned. There was a growing demand for pomp and ceremony in processions, pilgrimages and church celebrations. In the second half of the fifteenth century, in contrast – or perhaps to ease their consciences – wealthy burghers used to bring friars from mendicant orders inside the city walls.
They felt that they were fulfilling their religious duties by giving money to these monks with their unworldly way of life.

In the fifteenth century there was a religious revival in the German countries, which advocated a return to a purer perception of religion and increasingly opposed the malpractices which, far from being discouraged, were openly tolerated by Rome. Yearning for a stronger, more personal belief and condemning the accumulation of church functions, the sale of offices and letters of indulgence, Martin Luther decided to publish his reformist ideas in 95 theses in 1517, The Reformation had started. It soon found favour in the Netherlands. Central government was opposed to religious variety as it only led to political unrest. In 1521 it issued the first edict against the Reformation in 1521 and ordered Jan de Bakker to be burnt at Woerden in 1525, to set an example.
These reactions also stemmed from the fact that a much more aggressive movement than peace-loving Lutheranism had risen in southern Germany, which appealed to the lower classes in particular. Known as Anabaptism, it spread rapidly over northwestern Europe. John Beukels of Leiden, one of the leading anabaptists in the Netherlands, also led the conquest of the city of Münster where the anabaptists maintained a 'Kingdom of God' for almost a year. Everywhere followers of this social revolutionary movement were persecuted fiercely by the authorities, especially after an attempt to set up a similar community in Amsterdam had failed. Anabaptism is not to be confused with the baptist faith which was also persecuted, although it was of a more peaceable nature. This religion had many followers in Friesland where it was preached by Menno Simons.
Calvinism was called after John Calvin, who preached his ideas in Geneva. His doctrine did not spread widely in the Netherlands until after 1550, when it became the foremost Protestant movement there.

From the beginning, Charles V was in favour of taking severe action against Protestantism in all his states; as early as 1522 he consulted with the pope on a reorganization of the episcopal sees, to make Church policy more efficient. However, most of his subjects saw this as another intolerable example of centralized power that undermined the independence of the various states, and it was not realized during his rule. However, in 1555 a Peace of Religion was signed at Augsburg, which decreed that all through the dozens of states that formed the Holy Roman Empire, the religion of a ruler was to be shared by his subjects. This meant that the seventeen states that were referred to as the Netherlands would be obliged to remain Roman Catholic.

The 'Hay-wain' by Hieronymus Bosch (c. 1450-1516), as it accompanies the souls of the damned on their way to hell

Martin Luther (1483-1546), originally an Augustine monk, who protested against abuses in the Roman Catholic Church. Together with other reformers he laid the foundations of Protestantism

John Calvin (1509-1564), the reformer from Geneva whose teachings found a large following in the Netherlands after 1550 ▶

IOANNES CALVINUS

Society and politics after 1550; growing opposition to 'Spanish' rule

In 1549, Charles V issued the Pragmatic Sanction. In it he decreed that a single law of inheritance would be followed in all the seventeen Netherlands, ensuring their indivisible heritage under one ruler, to be confirmed by the Holy Roman Emperor as the Netherlands' suzerain. The seventeen states' assemblies ratified the Sanction after which Philip, Charles' son, made his entrance in the Netherlands to be honoured as the Emperor's successor in all the states. He toured the seventeen capitals, being received with much pump and circumstance, and through a wide array of propagandistic means proclaimed his right to rule by Divine law. At the same time, the regional elites tried to assert their continued role in state government by asking him to confirm their privileges.

King Philip II (1527-1598)

In 1555, Philip duly took over the government from his father. Charles retired to a Spanish monastery where he died three years later. Also in 1555, his governor-general, Mary of Hungary, had left her post to be succeeded by a new governor in the years to follow. But as long as Philip resided in the Netherlands to supervise war with France, he was able to govern in person.
The administration continued as before with the Council of State as the main advisory body in name, headed by Antoine Perrenot, later Cardinal Granvelle, a highly influential civil servant. Besides five senior legal officials, the Council comprised a number of major aristocrats including the Counts of Lalaing and of Egmond, as well as William of Nassau, who stemmed from one of the Empire's leading families, but had extensive properties in the Netherlands as well as being ruler of Orange, an independent principality to the south of France.
However, rather than ruling with these magnates, Philip preferred to consult a few trusted advisors. Disregarded, the majority of the mighty nobles in the Council of State, found this extremely frustrating. So did the Prince of Orange, who had been a favourite at the court of Charles V. Though he had befriended the later Cardinal Granvelle, he fell from grace when, in 1561, against Granvelle's advice he married Anna of Saxony, the wealthy daughter and heiress of one of Charles's old enemies.

◀ *Philip II (1527-1598), Lord of the Netherlands, King of Spain, A portrait by Antonio Moro*

Cardinal Granvelle

When Philip left the Netherlands in 1559, Granvelle gradually assumed effective power, to the displeasure of Margaretha of Parma, the king's half-sister, who ruled in her brother's place. In the mean time, several of the major nobles had been named the King's lieutenants, or 'stadholders' in the main provinces, among them William of Orange, who assumed the lord-lieutenantship of Holland, Zeeland, West-Frisia and Utrecht. Yet, Granvelle increasingly excluded many of these members of the Council of State from its consultations. Moreover, there was another way in which Granvelle was able to influence the administration. In 1559, the long-awaited reorganization of the Church hierarchy of the Netherlands had been effectuated. All new dioceses were placed under the supervision of the Archbishop of Mechlin, who also became the spokesman for the clergy in the States of Brabant. Formerly this had been a privilege of the abbot of the great abbey of Affligem. In view of its great wealth, this abbey had been incorporated in the diocese, thus enabling the archbishop to enjoy the privileges of the abbot. The newly-appointed Archbishop of Mechlin was none other than Granvelle, who now acquired a double hold on the government of the Netherlands.

The League of the peers: the Prince of Orange and other nobles

In 1562, the dissatisfied court nobles formed a League under the leadership of William of Orange. They demanded that the King recall Granvelle, who had been made a cardinal in the meanwhile. They succeeded because Margaretha had her own reservations about Granvelle's performance. The King gave in. On the pretext of a family visit, the cardinal left the Netherlands in 1564, never to return. While his departure gave the nobles more influence in the administration, they were not satisfied, yet, because the seventeen states were in a state of economic depression. This was partly a result of the costly wars waged by Charles V which Philip II was continuing. To finance these wars, Charles had borrowed heavily at high rates of interest. Though Spain provided the Netherlands with funds from the proceeds of its South-American gold and silver, the Dutch were nevertheless convinced that their tax moneys were often used in wars which were of no importance to the Netherlands, but only served the aggrandizement of the Habsburg family. As taxation rose drastically, it was borne under increasing protest and the King's attempts to introduce a capital levy on trade and industry were rejected resolutely by the States-General. After all, the representatives of the cities often were businessmen themselves.

The first signs of revolt

Since 1563, the economic situation had been deteriorating even further for most of the population. The Sound was closed yet again during a war between Sweden and Denmark. Both merchant shipping and transports of grain from the Baltic, a lifeline of food, became impossible. When the harvest also failed, after an unusually severe winter, the people were in a mood for revolt.

Uprisings were not at all unusual among various groups of the Netherlands' population. During the long period of the states' independence most of the cities had gained privileges which they intended to keep. If these were threatened a town would often rise in revolt against the duke or count who was usually obliged to give in, because he could not afford to antagonize his tax-paying burghers.
One of these regional privileges was the administration of justice. In most states, the people objected to a central jurisdictional body such as the Parliament of Mechlin. But they objected even more strongly to the Inquisition introduced by Charles V to deal with the persecution of the protestants, considered to be heretics, and with other dissidents. Although in most states people were well aware that religious differences caused trouble, they saw persecution by the central government as interference with their own authority. It filled them with dismay to see fellow townspeople tortured or burned at the stake in Brussels, or in the state's capital. As a result, in Holland no heretics were burned after 1553 and the death sentence became rare in Friesland.
In the 1560's the difficult financial and economic situation, combined with religious persecution and political unrest caused feelings to run high.
An important factor was that from 1560 onwards the protestants, partly Lutheran,

William the Silent (1533-1584) Count of Nassau, Prince of Orange, became leader of the revolt in the Netherlands. A portrait attributed to A. Th. Key, c. 1579 (Public Information Service RVD) ▶

partly Calvinist, had established a more efficient organization. In this, they were influenced by the large numbers of Calvinist refugees who had fled France to escape religious persecution, there. These Huguenots, who had well-organized communities themselves, now helped organize them in the Netherlands, too. Within a few years the far stricter doctrines of John Calvin almost replaced the more moderate forms of Protestantism such as Lutheranism.

The 'Compromise' of the lesser nobility

Calvinism had its followers among all ranks of the population. A number of the lesser nobility also sympathized with it or had joined one of its churches. Like the court nobles, these lesser nobles were dissatisfied with the way central government operated. Many felt their privileged position was undermined, both economically and militarily, what with heavy taxation and the introduction of mercenar armies. As the court nobles, they decided to co-operate and formed their own league called the "Compromise"; they presented Margaretha with a petition asking her to abolish the Inquisition. This was a deed aimed at a hated symbol, just as it was a sign of revolt to embrace Calvinism. Signed by over 400 lesser nobles, the petition was delivered by 200 armed men on 5 April 1566. On that occasion, Berlaymont, a member of the Council of State, is said to have told the governor-general disparagingly that the men were beggars only, or 'gueux' in French. The nobles were quick to adopt the Dutch form, proudly calling themselves 'geuzen'.

Two court nobles, the Lords of Montigny and Bergen, travelled to Spain to present the petition to the King. For while Margaretha's reaction had been favourable, promising that no one would be persecuted for his beliefs, her decision had to meet with the King's approval.

Still, Margaretha's promise did not entirely satisfy the Calvinists who also wanted the freedom to worship openly. As a form of provocation, they held services in the open air, which sometimes were attended by over a thousand people. As it soon became customary to go armed to these services, to be able to defend oneself against government officials, this tended to be seen as a political, rather more than a religious manifestation; an atmosphere of rebellion soon prevailed.

The destruction of the images

Meanwhile, rumour had it that some of the leading nobles had converted to the Reformation, too, thereby committing heresy. Egmond, Hoorne and Orange were among those suspected. They resented this bitterly and announced their intention of leaving the Netherlands, to the displeasure of Margaretha, who needed them to calm the Calvinists. Although she was successful in persuading them to stay for the time being, the storm could no longer be averted, especially in the South of Flanders, that was in the grip of a deep depression. There was general unrest, as a result of a shortage of food because the Sound had frozen over and of unemployment in the textile industry due to the falling supply of wool from England. In August 1566, an iconoclastic fury broke out, causing irreparable damage in many churches; especially, sculpted representations of saints, and other symbols of the hated official Church – associated with a repressive government – were removed, to prepare the churches for Protestant worship which did not allow images.

Pressed by these circumstances, Margaretha granted the Calvinists permission to openly worship their religion in those areas where they were already held secretly. This satisfied the lesser nobles who now promised to support the governor-general in maintaining order. Most of the major nobles also rallied to her side although some of them favoured military intervention.

The renewed oath of allegiance to the King

At the beginning of 1567, the members of the famous Order of the Golden Fleece, which had been devised by the Burgundian dukes to foster some spirit of unity among the leading aristocracy of their many states, together with the senior government officials and officers were asked to renew their oath of allegiance to King Philip II. Some of the leading nobles, including Orange and Hoorne, refused to do so. Hoorne later complied, but in May, when the situation deteriorated, Orange fled to Germany together with thousands of other rebels, most of them Calvinists.
Some of the most rebellious figures and the many whose possessions had been confiscated took to the sea to continue the rebellion as 'Sea Beggars'.

Alba and the Council of Blood

At her wits' end, the governor-general resigned her post in the same year. Her rather panicky account of the situation led Philip to raise an army of 10,000 men which entered the Netherlands on 22 August 1567, led by Don Fernando Alvarez de Toledo, Duke of Alba. Philip gave Alba almost unlimited power to act as his new governor-general. One of the Duke's first decisions was to set up the Council of Troubles, soon commonly known as the Council of Blood on account of the death sentences it pronounced.
The King's rigorous action, prompted by exaggerated reports of the situation, probably caused the Calvinistic part of the Dutch population finally to reject his authority, or rather that of his hated representatives. William of Orange, or the Silent, as he now became known, also suffered personal loss at Alba's hands. His eldest son and heir, Prince Philip-William, named after the King, who was a student at Louvain, was abducted and held hostage in Spain, never to see his father again. The fellow-campaigners of Orange too, Egmond and Hoorne, were taken prisoner and even executed in 1568.

The arrival of the Duke of Alba at Rotterdam, as recreated by the 19th- century French painter Isabey
© Photo RMN

Decades of strife

1568: the beginning of a war that would last for 'eighty years'

Meanwhile in the German countries, the Prince of Orange had raised four small armies of mercenaries which were to invade the Netherlands under his own leadership and that of his brothers, the other Counts of Nassau. In May, 1568, a battle was fought at Heiligerlee in Groningen, and Philip's stadhouder for Friesland was defeated, but Adolph of Nassau was killed. Two months later this small army, now under Louis of Nassau, was defeated once more, now by Alba himself.

Prince William's own invasion of Brabant, in the autumn of 1568, also failed. He was compelled to retreat to Germany, disbanding his armies due to lack of funds.

When making his plans Orange had counted on support from the people. But however rebellious their mood, they were still not desperate enough to follow the Prince in violently challenging the policies pursued in the King's name; whether Orange, at that time, had any other, more far-reaching plans, is uncertain.

The situation changed when, in addition to his persecution of the Calvinists, Alba introduced new tax measures. These met with widespread opposition although they were very sensible, aiming at a more proportional distribution of the fiscal burden over the population. Especially merchants and entrepreneurs – the urban elite – objected to Alba's plan to levy a sales' tax of 10% on all transactions, known as the Tenth penny. Apart from the blow this would deal to business, it would also weaken the power of the purse of the States-General and thus its leverage vis à vis the government, because these fiscal measures were meant to be permanent.

Although the States-General bought off their obligation to pay the Tenth penny for the first two-year period, in 1571 Alba made a fresh attempt to levy the tax, albeit in a milder form. He now met with resistance not only from the town councils, but also from such hitherto loyal members of the Council of State as Berlaymont. At this point Alba resigned, but the King asked him not to leave before he had restored law and order.

1572: The capture of Brill

Meanwhile, William of Orange had realized that he might as well profit from the growing opposition, and had raised a new army, with the support of the French Protestants who were more than willing to combat the Spaniards their arch-enemy. However, his plan to attack the government troops from the south and the east failed miserably. The Sea Beggars, who were campaigning to occupy some of the important coastal towns of Holland and Zeeland, were more successful. On 1 April 1572, they captured Brill, in the same month taking Vlissingen and Veere as well. At last the revolt which the Prince had hoped for earlier broke out in Holland, of which he still claimed to be the King's lieutenant.

Most of the towns rallied to his side with a few exceptions, including Amsterdam, that feared for its commercial interests.

Meanwhile, Alba was campaigning against an army commanded by Louis of Nassau in the south, so that he was unable to crush the revolt.

An assembly of the revolutionary towns at Dordrecht elected William of Orange as 'Stadhouder', which meant that he still represented the King's authority: they thus upheld the fiction that the King, of course, was well-intentioned towards his seventeen Netherlands, but that his representatives in Brussels were misinforming him, thus causing him to endorse a bad policy. At first, the rebels did not intend to withdraw their allegiance to the King, as they eventually did; they only demanded that their rights and privileges be acknowledged and that the interests of the Netherlands would no longer be subservient to Spanish policy. In a popular battle song written at this time – which only in the twentieth century was promoted to the status of Dutch National Anthem – William's own words were given as: 'I have always honoured the King of Spain'.

At first the revolt seemed to spread from its starting point in Holland to the other provinces. Parts of Friesland and Gelderland were won over to the side of the Prince. But the Massacre of St. Bartholomew's Eve in Paris, on 24 August 1572, during which countless Huguenots were betrayed and murdered by their Catholic countrymen, put an end to favourable developments. Without financial aid from France the Prince of Orange was forced once more to disband his army. He withdrew to Holland, the province which had been the first to support him.

1573 and 1574: the relief of Alkmaar and Leiden

Alba took revenge by sending an army to plunder some of the rebellious towns. After an unsuccessful siege of Alkmaar the Spanish troops had to retreat. Water, so often the enemy of the Dutch, came to their rescue now. The land surrounding the town was inundated by cutting the dykes, and this forced the besieging army to retreat. This event took place on 8 October 1573 and it is still celebrated in Alkmaar today as the first rebel victory.

Skirmishes continued, though. A year later, on 3 October 1574, Leiden was taken by the rebels. In 1575, to thank God, the first university to be founded in the northern Netherlands was established here, for the purpose of training Protestant ministers. Meanwhile, the Prince of Orange had joined the Calvinist Church and at least in Holland the tide had turned to such an extent that the provincial States now prohibited Roman Catholic worship altogether.

1576: The Pacification of Ghent

Don Louis de Requesens, appointed governor-general after the departure of Alba in 1573, attempted to reach an agreement with rebellious Holland at a conference in Breda, but without success. He died suddenly in 1576 after which the Spanish troops, who had not been paid for some time, advanced on Brabant and Flanders. They brutalized the population, looting and raiding the country and threatening the towns. With royal, Spanish authority temporarily absent, the Council of State now took over the government. In defiance of the King the States-General were convened at Ghent where a 'Pacification' or peace treaty was signed.
In the Pacification of Ghent the Netherlands provinces were pledged to co-operate in ending the 'Spanish Fury'. However, no definite solution was found for the growing religious differences. Still, the laws on persecution of heretics were suspended and Catholics outside Holland and Zeeland were to be left in peace.
The ideal which Orange had cherished over the years seemed to have been achieved; in spite of religious differences the Netherlands were united against Spanish politics and Spanish methods and there was a certain degree of religious tolerance.

1579: The Union of Arras and the Union of Utrecht

It now seemed as if the rebellion gained ground in the Southern Netherlands as well. William of Orange was even brought to Brussels in triumph. But a number of Catholic nobles resisted the rise of Calvinism and joined forces under

1578: William of Orange and Archduke Matthias of Austria swear allegiance to Philip II and the States General

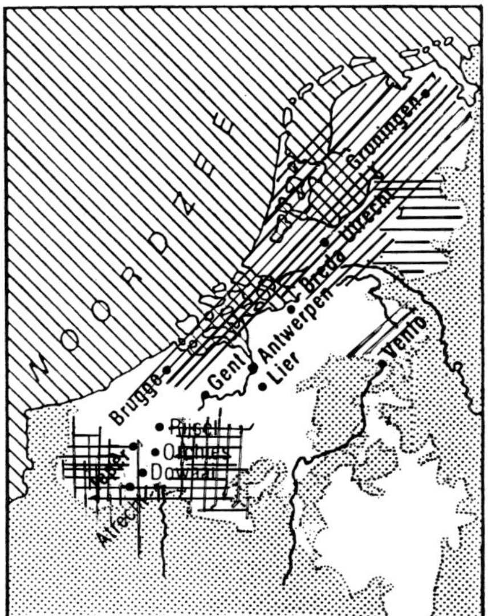

1579: the division of the Netherlands. A map of the Union of Utrecht and the Union of Arras. The Union of Utrecht included Holland, Zeeland, Friesland, the Groningen 'Ommelanden', Drenthe, three of the four quarters of Gelderland, Utrecht en the 'Freedom' of Bruges. The regions which formed a pact with the Union were: Overijssel and the County of Zutphen. The Union of Arras included Artois and Hainault

Montigny. They sided with Philip II, forming the Union of Arras on 6 January 1579. This amounted to a declaration of allegiance to the king and to the Roman Catholic religion. In reaction to this, on 23 January 1579 the Union of Utrecht was proclaimed, a pact between a number of the northern provinces with the object of continuing the struggle against Spain. It was signed by Holland, Zeeland, Utrecht and the Groningen county regions. William's brother, Count John of Nassau signed for Gelderland; Zutphen only joined after some hesitation, followed by Drenthe and Overijssel. In the act of Union it was agreed that the participating states were to remain united in a 'perpetual' alliance, and 'as if they were one', but that, on the other hand, each state was to retain its historically acquired rights. Important decisions such as declarations of war or peace and the introduction of tax measures were only to be agreed unanimously. In religious matters, each state had the right to decide for themselves, although it was understood that there was to be no further religious persecution.

1581: The Act of Abjuration – the Northern Netherlands declare their independence

The Prince of Orange, who supported the Union initiated mainly by his brother John, was formally outlawed by Philip in 1580. Consequently he advised the States-General to elect a new sovereign in the person of the French King's brother, the Duke of Anjou. Nor he, nor the other rebels could envisage a state or, as in this case, a federation of states which would not have their own ruler, as was normal in almost all other states of Europe; moreover, in selecting Anjou, he hoped to engage French support against Spain. Meanwhile, he himself would stay in power in Holland and Zeeland.

The natural sequel to this transfer of sovereignty was the Act of Abjuration of 22 July 1581, in which the States-General of the northern provinces, now assembled in The Hague, withdrew their allegiance from Philip II.

Anjou's appointment soon proved a symbolic act, only. In fact, government was in the hands of William of Orange and the States-General. The various states, or provinces, which retained their sovereignty, were governed by their Provincial States.

1584: The assassination of William of Orange

On 10 July 1584, William of Orange was assassinated at Delft, at the age of 51, by a man called Balthasar Gerards. The revolt had lost its leader. This may well have taught the provinces united in the Union of Utrecht to pull together. The States-General decided to entrust a Council of State with the administration of the union for the time being. Prince Maurice, the 17 year-old elder son of William of Orange, was made a member of the Council. In Friesland, John of Nassau, the son of one of William's brothers, was elected to become the new Stadhouder.

Meanwhile, the notion that a state could manage without the authority of a personal sovereign had not yet occurred to the leading politicians of the Netherlands. For this reason, on the death of Anjou, sovereignty was offered first to the King of France himself, who refused it, and then to Queen Elizabeth of England. She promised to send someone suitable for the position of governor-general. Her choice fell on her favourite, the Earl of Leicester who was appointed in 1586. His overbearing performance during the two years of his stay in the Netherlands did not impress the new leaders – least so the young, but ambitious Prince Maurice.

But after his departure, the future for the budding confederation looked bleaker than ever. In Autumn, 1588, a huge Spanish fleet – an Armada which King Philip thought

PLACCAERT

Vande Statẽ generael vande ghevnieerde Nederlanden:

BYDEN WELCKEN, MIDTS DEN REDENEN IN'T LANGE IN'T SELFDE begrepen, men verclaert den Coninck van Spaegnien vervallen vande Ouerheyt ende Heerſchappije van deſe voorſ. Nederlanden, ende verbiet ſijnen naem ende zeghel inde ſelue Landen meer te ghebruycken, &c.

SCRVTA-  MINI.

TOT LEYDEN,

By Charles Silvius / gheſwooren Drucker der Staten s'landts van Hollandt.

M. D. LXXXI.

Met privilegie voor tvvee jaren.

PLACCAERT VANDE STATEN GENERAEL VANDE ghevnieerde Nederlanden, Bijden welcken, mits den redenen in't langhe in't ſelfde begrepen, men verclaert den Coninck van Spaegnien vervallen vande Ouerheit eñ heerſchappije van deſe voorſ. Nederlanden : ende verbiet ſijnen naem ende zegel inde ſelue Landen meer te gebruycken, &c.

DE Staten generael vande ghevnieerde Nederlanden / Allen den ghenen die deſe teghenwoordige ſullen ſien ofte hooren leſen / ſaluyt. Alſo een yegelick kennelick is / dat een Prince vandẽ Lande van Godt gheſtelt is hooft ouer ſijne onderſaten / om de ſelue te bewaren eñ beſchermen van alle ongheluck / ouerlaſt eñ ghewelt / ghelijck een Herder tot bewaerniſſe van ſijne Schapen : Eñ dat d'onderſaten niet en zijn van Godt gheſchapen tot behoef vanden Prince / om hem in alles wat hy beveelt / weder het goddelic oft ongoddelick / recht oft onrecht is / onderdanich te weſen / eñ als ſlauen te dienen : maer den Prince om d'onderſaten wille / ſonder de welcke hy egheen Prince en is / om de ſelue met recht eñ redene te regeeren / ende voor te ſtaen eñ lief te hebben als een vader ſijne kinderen / eñ een herder ſijne ſchapen / die ſijn lijf eñ leuen ſett om de ſelue te bewaren. Eñ ſo wanneer hy ſulcks niet en doet / maer in ſtede van ſijne onderſaten te beſchermen / de ſelue ſoeckt te verdrucken / t'ouerlaſten / heure oude vrijheit / priuilegien / eñ oude herkomen te benemen / eñ heur te gebieden ende gebruycken als ſlauen /

A ij moet

Title-page and first page of the 'Act of Abjuration' published by Charles Silvius, Leiden, 1581

The tomb of William the Silent in the Nieuwe Kerk, Delft: it has been the family vault of the Oranges ever since.

invincible – was plying its way to the Netherlands to crush the rebellion once and for all and also to teach England a lesson. Fortunately for the rebel provinces the Armada was defeated off the coast of England, thanks to the bold action of Admiral Francis Drake, and its remnants were almost completely destroyed by a storm.

The 'Republic of the Seven United Provinces' on its way to independence

Prince Maurice and John van Oldenbarnevelt

It was mainly due to the efforts of two emerging key figures, Prince Maurice and John van Oldenbarnevelt, that an 'ad hoc' independent federation survived as a permanent 'Republic of Seven United Provinces'. Van Oldenbarnevelt (1547-1619) was the senior civil servant of Holland, authorized to sign resolutions on its behalf. Soon after the death of William the Silent, he persuaded the States of Holland to elect Prince Maurice as lord-lieutenant, or 'Stadhouder' – a rather strange construction, for the person whose place he was supposed to hold, King Philip of Spain, had been formally forsworn. In fact, one must assume that he was supposed to personify the authority of the actual sovereigns, the provincial States themselves; it indicates that, slowly, the awareness was growing that the Northern Netherlands were a confederation of seven republics, which, in international parlance, now came to be called the Republic of the Seven United Dutch Provinces; however, they still needed someone to exercise a number of quasi-monarchical tasks.

Prince Maurice, who was a very competent military leader, also assumed the function of captain-general of the entire Republic's army. In the ongoing war against Spain, he won many campaigns, together with his cousin William Louis, Stadhouder of Friesland. Maurice's campaigns came to a halt in 1595 as the States-General lacked funds to pay the troops. But in 1596 both France and England were at last prepared to support the United Provinces and even to acknowledge them as an independent federation. In June of the same year Van Oldenbarnevelt succeeded in uniting the Northern Netherlands with France and England in the Triple Alliance.

The Twelve Years' Truce 1609-1621

In the year of his death, 1598, Philip II granted the Netherlands to his daughter Isabella on the occasion of her marriage to the new governor-general, her cousin Archduke Albert of Austria. In Spain the climate was ripe for a change of policy towards the situation in the Netherlands: the government in Madrid began to realize that it simply lacked the financial resources to pay for an interminable succession of annual campaigns, and that the interest on the money borrowed for this purpose was crippling Spain.

In the breakaway northern provinces, two trends in their attitude to Spain gradually emerged. One was for continuing efforts to win over the remainder of the seventeen Netherlands to the Revolt, the other was satisfied with the status quo.
Prince Maurice was the leader of the first group. He had his reasons for wanting to continue the war, partly out of self-interest. His one position of real power was that of captain-general of the army. Without a war this title would lose its meaning and the Prince would lose much of his power.
Van Oldenbarnevelt led the movement for peace in which he represented the views of most of the authorities in the towns of Holland. These 'regents' usually came from leading merchant families and saw no gain in an alliance with the southern provinces, particularly Flanders with its wealthy trading towns. Trade and industry were just beginning to prosper in the north, partly as a result of their decline in the south – no wonder these regents were quite content to continue to blockade the Scheldt River, the lifeline of Amsterdam's greatest competitor, Antwerp.
Still, many of the merchants favoured con-

tinuing the war which they thought had brought them prosperity. Calvinist zealots were also for continuing the struggle against Catholic Spain, in the Catholic south.

In 1609, Oldenbarnevelt succeeded in concluding a Twelve Years' Truce with Isabella and Albert, obviously against the wish of Prince Maurice. There were to be no hostilities during this period and the status quo was to be maintained, both in Europe and abroad, in the Indies, where the two camps had been competing as well. On behalf of King Philip III of Spain, the Archduke and his wife also agreed to acknowledge the sovereignty of the Republic during the truce.

Arminians and Gomarians

The opposing political views held by Prince Maurice and John van Oldenbarnevelt at the beginning of the Twelve Years' Truce were aggravated by religious differences. In 1603, a certain Protestant minister, Arminius had been named professor of theology at Leiden. He held fairly liberal views, particularly on the much-discussed tenet of predestination, a cornerstone of Calvinist doctrine which holds that salvation is foreordained by God for some and not for others. It was not long before Arminius came into conflict with Gomarus, also a Leiden professor, who held equally strongly but opposing to this vital issue.
Both theologians soon had their own followers among the ministers and the faithful. In 1610, a year after the death of Arminius, one of his followers presented a 'remonstrance' against predestination to the States-General, in the absence of a supreme ecclesiastical authority. This was answered by a counter-remonstrance from the Gomarians in 1611.

The States-General, who had no use for religious differences in the provinces, convened the two parties for a conference, but they would not be reconciled. Over the following years, the conflict deepened with Van Oldenbarnevelt supporting the tolerant Remonstrants (the moderates), and Prince Maurice taking the side of the Counter-Remonstrants (the strictly orthodox). The States of Holland chose the side of Van Oldenbarnevelt and the Remonstrants, relieved as they were that this group acknowledged temporal authority as the supreme power in religious matters as well. This did not suit the city council of Amsterdam which remained orthodox to demonstrate its political independence to the other towns of Holland.

The Synod of Dort 1618-1619

Oldenbarnevelt increasingly believed that the civil government should indeed have the last word in religious matters if it were to avoid great civil disturbance; it was thanks to him that the States of Holland passed the "Sharp Resolution" in 1617, refusing to convene a national synod to deal with the problems. They feared that the other provinces would use this religious issue as a pretext to voice their increasing uneasiness over Holland's growing economic and political preponderance in the federation; if the other states united on this point, they might be able to subject Holland to their political will.
Van Oldenbarnevelt also advised the town councils of Holland to employ a force of 'waardgelders', mercenaries, to deal with rioters. As the 'waardgelders' were to replace the regular troops led by Prince Maurice, he regarded Oldenbarnevelt's advice as a direct attack on his authority as captain-general. Of course, the conclusion of the Truce with Spain, a decade earlier, had already started the process in which the two of them had drifted apart.

As was to be expected, the majority of the provinces in the States-General took the side of the Prince against Holland. In 1618 they decided to hold a national synod after all,

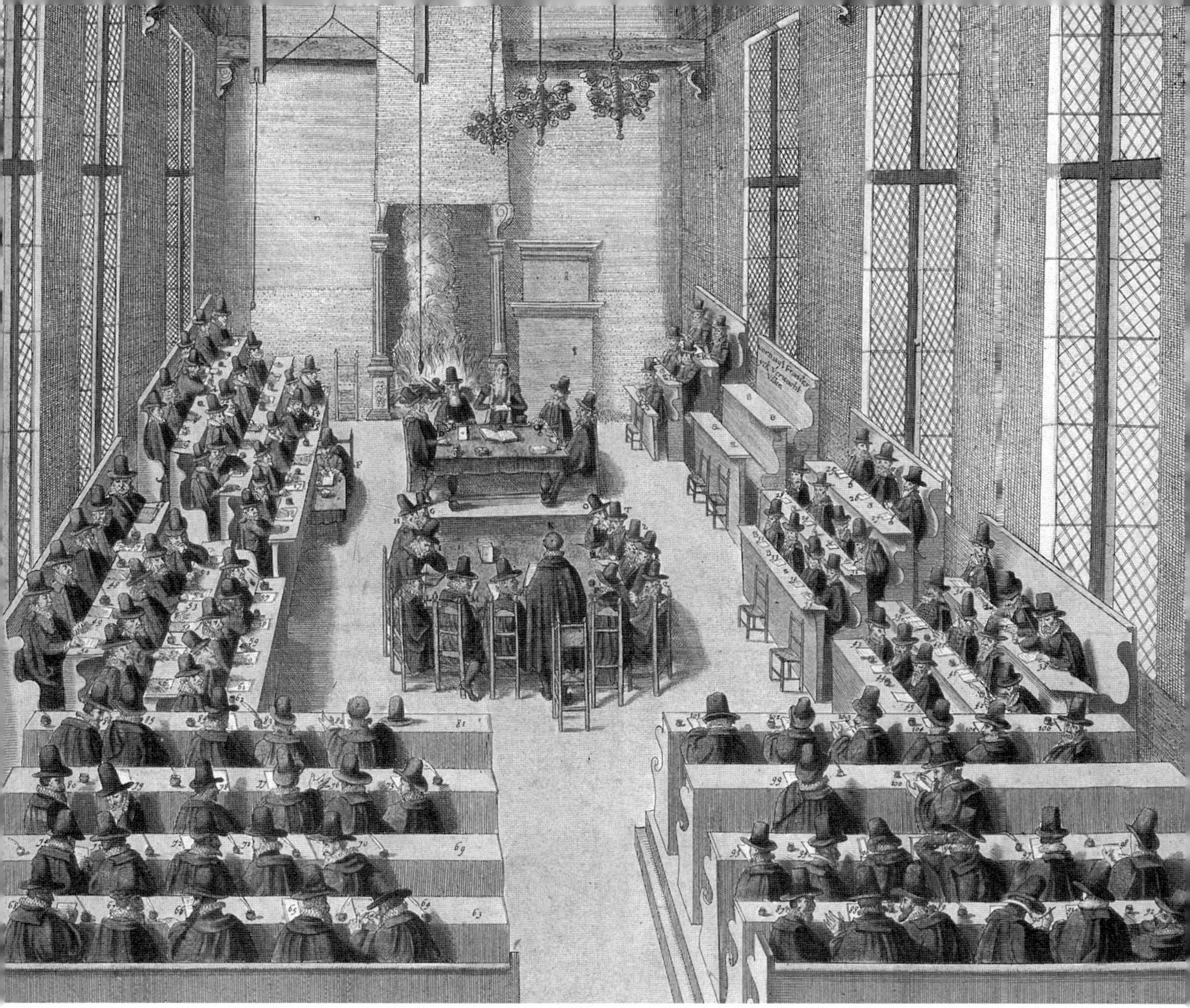

Anonymus engraving showing the Synod at Dordrecht, November 13, 1618 (Atlas van Stolk)

which met at Dordrecht. The Remonstrant doctrines were denounced and Calvinist orthodoxy was formulated precisely. A new translation of the Bible was also ordered. Completed in 1637, it was called the 'States' Bible'; to many Protestants, this was the only true Word until well into the twentieth century.

For the time being, the Remonstrant preachers continued their struggle in secret; however, already by 1630 their meetings were tolerated as before. Many of the regents preferred the tolerant Remonstrants to the more fanatical Counter-Remonstrants, who were averse to the power of temporal government and would have preferred something of a theocracy.

The execution of John van Oldenbarnevelt

Meanwhile Prince Maurice had taken high-handed action in several cities, replacing regents who sided with Van Oldenbarnevelt or the Remonstrants. The States-General

The surrender of Breda to the Spanish commander Spinola in 1625, as depicted on the famous painting 'Las Lanzas' by the Spanish artist Diego Velasquez

condoned this action and in 1618 gave him full power, on which he ordered the imprisonment of Van Oldenbarnevelt and his associates.
The subsequent trial of Van Oldenbarnevelt – much less than legally correct -, followed by his execution in May 1619, was the culmination of the political and religious differences which had developed in the young Republic. Van Oldenbarnevelt was convicted for his policies and for his efforts to have them observed. But in reality he was the victim of the wish of many, including, of course, Prince Maurice, that the power of the Stadhouder and the States- General should prevail over the independence of the individual provinces, especially that of mighty Holland which threatened to dominate the others.

After the death of Van Oldenbarnevelt, Prince Maurice was the foremost authority in the Republic. In 1620 he also became Stadhouder of Groningen and Drenthe. At the end of the Twelve Years' Truce in 1621, he eagerly continued his successful military campaigns in the south, including the relief of the besieged frontier town of Bergen op Zoom.

On his death in 1625, Maurice was succeeded by his half-brother Frederick Henry as Stadhouder in five of the seven provinces. Groningen elected his cousin Ernst Casimir, who was already Stadhouder in Friesland. Like Maurice, Frederick Henry continued to lead many successful campaigns. He won Den Bosch, Venlo, Roermond, Maastricht, Breda, Sas van Gent and Hulst for the Republic, which earned him the nickname 'Subduer of Cities'. These successes ensured that part of the southern provinces of Brabant and Limburg now were added to the Republic's territory; but the fact that they were mainly Catholic was to prove a problem.
At sea, a decisive victory over the Spaniards was won in 1639, when Admiral Maarten Tromp destroyed a second armada in English territorial waters. But an outright victory over the royal South by the Republic, or of the North by Spanish troops did not seem possible.

Statue of Grand Pensionary Johan van Oldenbarnevelt (1547-1619), The Hague

1648: the Peace of Münster – the end of the Eighty Years' War

After a number of unsuccessful efforts, in 1640 negociations were finally started for another truce between both Spain and the Republic. In Holland, and especially in Amsterdam, the leading politicians were beginning to realize that a continuation of the war would be harmful to trading interests; the other provinces, too, were war-weary: the Republic had accumulated a gigantic debt, which pressed heavily on the population. Spain, too, was confronted with empty coffers.
But it was not until 1646 that all the provinces agreed on the necessity for a truce and, perhaps, even a definitive peace. It was now that the complexity of decision making in a confederation of seven almost autonomous republics became patently obvious. In 1646, a delegation of the States-General arrived at Münster, where representatives from France, Spain and the German Emperor had already gathered. Two more years of talks were needed on matters such as the recognition of the sovereignty of the Netherlands, freedom for Dutch merchants to trade with the East and West Indies, and, urged rather half-heartedly by the Spaniards, freedom to worship Catholicism in the Republic.
The peace treaty was finally signed in 1648. Its most important clause was the recognition by the Spanish king of the United Netherlands as a free and sovereign country. This sovereignty was also acknowledged by the Holy Roman Emperor, until then nominally still the highest authority in the larger part of the Northern Netherlands, the eastern provinces.

Another vital clause was the one excluding the Spaniards from trade with areas in the East and West Indies which had been won for the Republic between 1598 and 1648. Even more important: the Scheldt was to remain closed to merchant shipping from the southern Netherlands; this ensured the position of Amsterdam as international port as Antwerp was no longer able to compete. Freedom of religion, as far as conscience was concerned, was accepted, but in reality open Catholic worship was prohibited.
The Treaty of Münster marked the end of the Eighty Years' War with Spain. It was the official seal on a situation which had arisen in 1579 when the rebellious provinces first signed the Union of Utrecht.

The political structure of the Republic

It was mainly due to the efforts of Van Oldenbarnevelt that the independent northern provinces had a well-organized administration, albeit a complex one; sovereignty lay with each of the seven provincial assemblies or States. According to the Union of Utrecht, their representatives in the States-General were responsible for 'war and peace', in short for the management of foreign affairs, to be decided upon unanimously. In the seven states, the cities carried great weight in the assemblies. They were governed by a 'vroedschap' or city council of wise ('vroede') men who appointed civic officials. Recruited, mostly, from the urban elite, these councils filled their own vacancies. This soon led to the formation of an oligarchic system: a small number of regent families called the tune. In the rural areas of most provinces, power usually lay with the families of landowners who were often nobles. With the urban representatives, they dominated the provincial States.

The seven provinces with the right to vote in the States-General were Holland, Zeeland, Utrecht, Friesland, Groningen, Overijssel and Gelderland; Drenthe also had a degree of provincial sovereignty. A rather different status had been given to the 'Generality Lands' as the states of Brabant, Vlaanderen and Limburg were called: they were governed not by independent assemblies but directly by the States-General in which they had no representation. Obviously, this was the result of having been conquered from the Spanish government in Brussels in the campaigns of the period ca. 1580-1640; they were considered as spoils of war. Another reason for this treatment was that Catholicism had a strong following in these areas and that there was much resentment against the enforced union with the northern provinces. In consequence, many Protestants from the North feared that these areas would eventually betray them.

Map of the Dutch Republic in 1648

The ratification of the 'Peace of Münster' (1648), painted by Gerard ter Borch ►

The economy of the Golden Age: the Republic as the centre of world trade

From the 1580's onwards, the economic situation in Holland and Zeeland was excellent; this was partly due to a stream of economically powerful or at least productive refugees form the South after the fall of Antwerp in 1585. It was not long before Amsterdam and Middelburg had taken over the role of Antwerp, previously the foremost trading centre of Europe. Not surprisingly, Holland made sure to keep the Scheldt closed to shipping until well into the eighteenth century.

During the first decades of the seventeenth century, the two sea-fronting states of the small Republic, developed into the centre of world trade, with Amsterdam at the hub. Several factors contributed to this situation. Firstly, the success of the fishing industry, and of international trade, also with its related industries, which had started growing in the preceding centuries. Secondly, the absence of a protectionist economic policy, due to the absence of a truly central government that, as in most other European countries, would be inclined to dominate the economy. Such a policy would not have fitted in the scheme of the seven autonomous little republics. Moreover, it was only natural that the leading merchants, who laid down the law in the government of Holland and Zeeland, carried out a foreign policy which promoted their own trade. Also, the Republic developed a well-functioning infrastructure as well as, at least in the cities, an educational system that resulted in one of the highest literacy rates in the world; both factors obviously favoured economic growth. Last, but not least, the existence of large amounts of natural fuel, especially peat, provided a boost to the economy.

The other five little republics, the 'land provinces', remained largely rural; in consequence, they did not enjoy the affluence which the sea provinces acquired during the seventeenth century. This was reflected in the tax revenues which were needed to finance the joint policy of the seven republics: Holland alone paid 58% of the total dues. The economic situation of the largely rural Generality Lands deteriorated because the States-General did not always act in their interest. One of the prosperous cities of former times to lose its affluence because of this policy was 's Hertogenbosch, captured in 1629.

Trade to the Baltic, the Strait and England

The Netherlands had long taken part in trade with the Baltic. Already in the second half of the sixteenth century, Amsterdam was the European centre for the grain trade. This, in turn, led to trade in all kinds of other commodities. Salt, wine and spices from southern Europe, as well as herring and textiles were shipped to the Baltic ports; Swedish copper was taken back on the return journey, to provide material for the arms' industry. Dutch traders also sailed to Russia, buying large quantities of fur and hides, as well as small but profitable quantities of caviar and gems. The Dutch merchant fleet was so active in trade with the Baltic that almost half of the ships which passed the tolls of the Sound before 1650 were Dutch-owned. Holland and Zeeland rightly regarded trade to the Baltic as the 'mother' of their commercial wealth.

In addition, the 'Straatvaart' or trade with southern Europe through the Straits of Gibraltar also flourished. Many of the commodities mentioned above were bought there but it was also important for export. Grain was exported mainly to Spain. Merchant shipping branched out after 1590 to find its way through the Straits to the

Meanwhile, all European powers indulged in such profitable privateering pastime, if only it harmed their enemies

Junctions of an empire: 'Holland on the Hudson' and the Brazilian failure.

There was also some colonization in the Americas, including the Windward Islands – still part of the kingdom of the Netherlands – and Brazil. The latter was highly important because it catered to Europe's growing need of such delicacies as tobacco and sugar. For some twenty years, the Dutch held the north-eastern part of Brazil, around Recife, which they conquered from the Portuguese; in the end, however, they had to relinquish their colony again. The 'Mauritshuis' at The Hague, today one of the Netherlands' foremost museums, was built with Brazilian gold by the last Dutch governor of the colony, Prince Maurice of Nasau-Siegen.

North America, which had not been colonized by the Spanish or Portuguese, lay open to other European conquerors from the late sixteenth century onwards. At the mouth of the Hudson, the Dutch established a colony-cum-trading post, which they used as a base from which to contact the Indian tribes who lived along the river, and who provided them with furs and hides. A number of Dutch families moved inland, creating several sometimes very extensive estates, or 'patroonships' from 1629 onwards. A number of names of cities and villages bear witness to this episode. Even the metropolis now known as New York was once founded on Manhattan island as New Amsterdam; it had its "wall", hence 'wall-street', and, nearby, another village called "Breukelen", hence 'Brooklyn' et cetera. In 1667, the English forced the Dutch to cede this colony as part of a peace settlement following a war they had won.

Actually, the West India Company never fully exploited the trading and other potential of this settlement, partly due to lack of vision, partly due to lack of capital. Indeed, the West India Company never achieved the stature of its East India counterpart.

Junctions of an empire: Surinam.

When the English claimed New Amsterdam to round off their North American colonies, the Dutch were not entirely unwilling to accept Surinam, on the Northeast coast of South America, in compensation. The region was thought to provide an entry into the gold reserves of the interior. Though by that time the first W.I.C. had gone bankrupt, it was re-established in another form and it now acquired Surinam, which was settled by Dutchmen, Huguenots from France, and Jewish refugees from the Iberian peninsula; mostly, they founded plantations, there, to produce sugar and other products for the European market. To cultivate the land, the Company imported numerous negro slaves from West Africa. To ensure a steady supply, the Dutch joined other European countries in the acquisition of slaves from African traders, with whom they dealt from a number of forts on the West Coast of Africa taken from the Portuguese in the early decades of the seventeenth century.

The rise of industry

In the seventeenth century, the flourishing of Dutch trade encouraged the rise of various industries. Shipbuilding boomed in the Zaan region and supply companies such as rope-yards and sailmakers did a roaring trade.

Trade also promoted processing industries, working with imported raw materials or semi-finished products as in sugar-refining. In addition to these trade-related industries, others also prospered as a result of the rapidly growing markets and, again, especially due to the arrival of refugees from the South, many of them skilled workers. The production of cloth by the textile industry at Leiden was at its height, stimulated by the skilled Flemish weavers who introduced modern methods. Meanwhile, the fame of this prospering industry also attracted labourers from the far less prosperous German regions that bordered on the Dutch Republic. Generally speaking, of course, labour and its price determined the ability of Dutch industry to compete on the European market; with growing taxes and the cost of labour rising as well, this very ability declined during the later decades of the seventeenth century.

Meanwhile, Holland and Zeeland were the provinces to benefit most from the prosperity which trade and industry brought, as did Friesland, to some degree. In the other provinces agriculture was still the main source of income; there, trade and industry maintained the same low level as in previous centuries, so that the contrast with the coastal provinces became steadily more marked.

The reclamation of land

The reclamation of land in the north of Holland was a direct result of the prosperity ensuing from trade and industry. It now became essential to increase the area under cultivation, if only to ensure that the rising population of Holland especially, did not become totally dependent on food imports, but, if possible, to produce a surplus for export as well. Many leading citizens invested their money in the reclamation business, like the famous poet and senior civil servant Jacob Cats, as well as such capitalists as Dirck van Os, an executive of the V.O.C. The Beemster, a large lake, was drained between 1608 and 1610 with the technical aid of Jan Adriaansz. Leeghwater and the energy provided by forty windmills. In the course of the next twenty-five years, 18,300 ha. of land was reclaimed by draining other polders in North Holland.

Stagnation or decline?

The climax of this period, during which the Republic dominated European world trade, lay between 1630 and 1650. The merchant fleet at that time consisted of over 2500 ships, with at least another 2000 fishing vessels, mostly herring 'busses'.

A very gradual decline set in after 1650, not so much affecting the prosperity of the Republic as its undisputed leading role in the world economy. England grew steadily stronger as a rival, but not before the prosperity of the western provinces of the Netherlands had stimulated the arts and sciences to blossom as never before.

Map from 1607, showing the great Beemster, Wormer and Schermer lakes that were reclaimed between 1612 and 1635

The civilization of the Dutch 'Golden Age'

The Dutch Republic as a 'burgher state'

The Republic was a polity and a society unlike most other European states in that it was steered at the highest level not by a monarch and an attendant nobility and clergy, but by a bourgeois elite. The influence of the burgher culture was particularly strong in the various forms of art. Back in the late fifteenth and early sixteenth century, the prosperous burghers had first competed with the nobility and clergy in commissioning works of art, mainly collectively, and usually in the form of commissioning a building or a piece of sculpture. Now, in the seventeenth century the part played by nobles and clergy in patronage of the arts was almost entirely taken over by the burghers.

The present Palace on the Dam, built in the 17th century as the Town Hall of Amsterdam by Jacob van Campen

Painting: genre pictures

Bourgeois patronage first and foremost became visible in painting. Even today people are amazed at the enormous quantity of qualitatively high-rank paintings produced in the Dutch Republic, and covering nearly all genres. In the seventeenth century, too, foreign visitors showed their surprise when they saw the amounts of paintings being offered for sale even on ordinary week-day markets and fairs; they also were astonished to note that even simple artisans and farmers owned such paintings.

This situation had a definite impact on the development of painting. In seventeenth-century Holland a unique style emerged, due to the many genre pictures which were painted because they appealed to the general public. The subjects were usually moralistic, in the spirit of the writer Jacob Cats, whose literary work was very popular partly because he advocated a judicious combination of business, acumen and soberness with the pleasure of life that greatly appealed to the pious yet art-loving middle classes.

Especially popular were the group portraits of the numerous boards of governors of commercial companies and civic institutions, which helped to express both pride and status. Famous examples of this kind were painted by Bartholomew van der Helst (1613-1670) and Frans Hals (1580-1666). The best-known painting of militiamen was a 'portrait' of the Company of Captain Frans Banning Cock which, in the romantic nineteenth century, was dubbed the most famous painting of the entire seventeenth century. Painted in 1642 by Rembrandt van Rijn (1606-1669) it is known as 'The Night Watch'.

Baroque (religious) art

In addition to genre painting and landscapes, seascapes and portraits which all catered to the taste of the wealthier burghers, there was also art for the aristocracy, and for the Catholics, now worshipping in private. This work was more ambitious in content and more sophisticated, in a cosmopolitan way, relating strongly to the international baroque style of painting that had developed in Italy. Artists working in this style usually came from the School of Utrecht, which was not surprising as this cathedral city remained staunchly Catholic even after the Reformation. This baroque style was accentuated when a number of artists came to Haarlem from Antwerp after it was captured. Jointly they worked towards that version of Baroque which is called Mannerism. The oldest member of this group was Karel van Mander (1548-1606), known for his 'Book of Artists' containing the biographies of some of the most famous Dutch artists of the time. Hendrick Goltzius (1558-1617) was a native of Haarlem, a skilled engraver who specialized in coloured wood prints. Work of this kind, more especially depicting scenes from the Bible, was often commissioned by wealthy Catholics for their 'secret' conventicles. Paintings by artists of the School of Utrecht were also in demand at the internationally-orientated court of Stadhouder Frederick Henry. His widow, Amalia van Solms, commissioned ambitious murals for the central room of 'Huis ten Bosch', the palace of the present queen at The Hague. In this so-called *Room of the Orange-family*, frescoes in truly grand, allegorical style highlighted scenes from the life of her husband who had died in 1647. Rembrandt, too, painted for the court. He was one of the few artists outside the Utrecht School to paint religious pictures. From his earliest days as a pupil the Bible had been a major source of inspiration.

Within this context, there is no room to further treat the variety of seventeenth-century Dutch painting. Gerard Ter Borch (1617-1681) is the one artist who deserves special mention here, not because his work was more remarkable than that of most of his fellow-artists, but because – of his own accord – he recorded one of the most momentous events in the history of the early Republic: he was the one to depict the Dutch and foreign diplomats in the act of ratifying the epochal Treaty of Münster, in 1648.

Architecture: the Renaissance and 'Dutch Classicism'

During the second half of the sixteenth century Renaissance elements began to cover architectural structures that were still medieval, gothic in essence. As yet, the ideal of Italian Renaissance architecture, the quest for perfect spatial dimensions in the right proportions – as embodied in the idealised human form – had not been taken up in the North.

By the year 1600, Hendrick de Keyser (1565-1621) and Lieven de Key (c. 1560-1617) were the two leading Dutch architects, employed by Amsterdam and Haarlem respectively. De Key was a refugee from the southern Netherlands and, like so many fellow artists, in high demand among his new compatriots. In the seventeenth century burghers took a more active part in commissioning buildings, both collectively and privately. Wealthy Amsterdam set the tone. After 1600, due to the rapidly increasing population, drastic expansion of the city became necessary. Between 1612 and 1672, the result was a series of new canals which, in three rings, called the Herengracht, Keizersgracht and the Prinsengracht, gave the city its characteristic image. Many lovely houses were built along the canals, including the famous 'Trippenhuis' designed by the architect Vingboons in a majestically-classical style for this enormously wealthy family of entrepreneurs and traders.

These canalside houses reflected the wealth and good taste of the merchant-regents, not only of Amsterdam and Holland, but also of Zeeland, Utrecht, Groningen and Friesland. Collectively they commissioned town halls and weighing houses and, also, churches. One of the most beautiful achievements in seventeenth-century civic Dutch architecture, the Town Hall of Amsterdam, was designed by Jacob van Campen (1595-1657). Construction started in 1648. The Town Hall has some typically Dutch characteristics. The architect worked in a restrained classical style that has been called Dutch Classicism. Still, with its sculptures and paintings that, together, form a grand, allegorical scheme that depicts Amsterdam in all its glory as the centre of world trade, it came to embody the ideal of the baroque: an integral work of art.

Literature: the Muider Circle

In literature, too, a tendency towards a specifically Dutch style of writing which already had set in during the sixteenth century, was evolving. One of the qualities for which the Dutch were known in the following centuries was tolerance towards dissidents – despite the fact that mercenary arguments played their part as well; this tolerance was illustrated in the work of Dirk Coornhert (1522-1590), a follower of Erasmus. The Eglantine Chamber of Rhetoric of Amsterdam did much to stimulate this. Hendrik Spiegel (1549-1612) and Pieter Roemer Visscher (1547-1620) were among its members. Their work is characterized by a moralizing view of the world, that was echoed in seventeenth-century painting.

The Amsterdam home of the merchant and poet Visscher was the venue for a large circle of painters, writers and singers, who included his daughters Anna and Maria Tesselschade. After his death, these gatherings took place in Muiden Castle which between 1610 and 1647 became a hub of cultural and scientific activity in the Republic. The variety of religious and political backgrounds represented in the so-called Muider Circle – which never was a real society – reflected the relatively tolerant social cli-

mate in the Dutch upper class during the seventeenth century. The fierce dispute between Remonstrants and Counter-Remonstrants had cast a shadow, but no lasting damage had been done.
Host to the Muider Circle was Pieter Cornelis Hooft (1581-1647). A burgomaster's son from Amsterdam, he had been appointed bailiff of Muiden by Prince Maurice in 1609. He wrote a number of plays, including a comedy called 'Ware-nar', an adaptation of a piece by the Roman writer Plautus. Hooft's methods were characteristic of the development of literature in the Netherlands. Towards the end of the sixteenth century, writers had been trying to find their own ways of expressing themselves; seventeenth-century authors increasingly found inspiration in the classics. As a historical writer, too, Hooft turned to ancient Rome for an example, when he started writing his great history of the early Dutch republic: Tacitus' *Annals* served as a model for Hooft's *Histories.*

Joost van den Vondel: the 'prince of poets'

Another text in the classical vein was the tragedy *Palamedes*, though it had a plot based on contemporary events, to wit the justicial murder of Oldenbarnevelt. Its author Joost van den Vondel (1587-1679), a Roman Catholic, also was a regular visitor to Muiden Castle. He, the greatest Dutch poet of that century, risked his life with this work which appeared in 1625. When the Amsterdam burgomasters, proud of the genius that adorned their town, let him off with a moderate fine, he wrote another tragedy, in defence of the Catholic Mary Stuart, Queen of Scots who had been beheaded by her Protestant rival Elisabeth. A comedy by Vondel, *'Leeuwendalers'*, was performed with great success at the Amsterdam Theatre to celebrate the Peace of Münster. The tragedy *Gijsbrecht van Aemstel* provided the people of Amsterdam with an inspiringly-written though historically inaccurate version of an early episode of their town's history, stressing its historic independence. Indicative of the true cosmopolitanism of a number of artists working in seventeenth-century Amsterdam is the fact that Vondel was among the very first European writers to base a literary text, and a play at that, on a non-European event: his tragedy *Zungchin* took place against the background of the recent, dramatic change of power in China. However, Vondel's most important plays undoubtedly are his biblical tragedies, of which *Lucifer* surely ranks among the greatest which was written in seventeenth-century Europe.

Hugo de Groot: founder of international law

Another visitor of the literary and musical gatherings at Muiden Castle was Hugo de Groot (1583-1645) or 'Grotius', a playwright, mathematician, theologian, historian and jurist. He was one of the political leaders of the Remonstrants, for which he was imprisoned in Loevestein Castle in 1619. He made a spectacular escape in a book chest, after which he was forced to live in exile His 'De Jure Belli ac Pacis libri tres' – 'three books on war and peace' – which appeared in 1625, laid the foundation for international law. In other writings he defended the freedom of the seas, and of international trade, hardly surprisingly in view of the fact that he was the head of the Dutch East India Company's legal department and thus wrote to pleasure his masters.

Music

There was music too, in Hooft's Muider Circle. Maria Tesselschade often introduced the Portuguese-Jewish singer Francisca Duarte, who then sang compositions set, to his own poems, by the statesman-poet-composer Constantine Huygens. Jan Pieterszoon Sweelinck (1562-1621), organist of the Old Church at Amsterdam was a welcome guest too. One of the greatest organ players and composers of his day, he had many German pupils. He invented the genre of the fugue which Johan Sebastian Bach later developed to perfection; he also wrote some beautiful vocal music mostly as a setting of the psalms.

Science and education

The transition to Protestantism had had far-reaching effects on education. The first university in the North, at Leiden, was founded with the precise object of providing adequate training facilities for protestant ministers. Other towns were eager to establish their own institutions of higher education in the wake of Leiden University, not only to show civic pride but to provide education to the elite of regents and wealthy merchants, beyond the level that could be reached at the traditional Latin schools. One such college was founded in Franeker in 1585, another in Utrecht in 1636 and yet another in Harderwijk in 1645.
One of the men who visited the meetings at Muiden, besides the many writers, musicians, lawyers and scholars was Gerardus Johannes Voss whose name was commonly Latinized as Vossius. He was professor of history at the 'Athenaeum Illustre', a college of higher education founded in Amsterdam in 1632 with standards on a par with those of Leiden university.

On the secondary level, too, there were some changes. Schools for middle-class children were started during the seventeenth century to provide more practical, commercial education. These were the 'French' schools, where the subjects taught were French, geography and arithmetic, besides, of course, in true Calvinist tradition, religious instruction and ethics. Most of the French schools were run privately, with boarding facilities for pupils living at a distance.
Of course, a knowledge of Latin, that had been and remained one of the mainstays of education at the Latin schools, was no longer necessary to take part in religious activities, as services were now conducted in Dutch. Moreover, as it was essential for the propagation of Calvinism that as many people as possible could read the Bible, this was printed in the vernacular, too. As a result so-called 'Dutch Schools' were founded everywhere, usually at the instigation of Church- or town-councils. Only the most elementary subjects such as reading and writing were taught at these schools. Even arithmetic was not part of the standard curriculum, though it seems that in the more commercially-orientated parts of the country this was soon introduced. However, all this educational activity did ensure that the rate of literacy in the Dutch Republic was among the highest in the contemporary

Society and politics in the second half of the seventeenth century

Stadhouder William II

After the Peace of Münster, England was the first to show hostile behaviour towards the Republic. Of course, trade rivalry had been endemic between the two regions since times immemorial, but now the Republic started on a more structured policy of economic expansion. One reason for the conflict that now ensued was that William II of Orange, Frederic Henry's only son, supported the cause of the English Stuarts who had been banished by Oliver Cromwell after the execution of Charles I in 1649. His stance was not surprising: he was married to the late king's daughter Mary.
Both for commercial and ideological reasons, most of the city regents were opposed to the Stadhouder's wish to intervene on behalf of the English royals.
Their relationship had cooled already after the Peace of Münster had been agreed against William's will. It did not improve when, in 1650, the States of Holland announced that they would no longer pay the 42 armed companies that were their share in the country's militia. William then caused a resolution to be passed by the States-General, ordering the captains to remain in charge of their companies. He forcefully visited the cities of Holland which had the right to vote in the provincial States. The opposition which met him wherever he went led him to imprison six leading regents in Loevestein Castle. Rebellious Amsterdam was even threatened by an army under William Frederick, Stadhouder of Friesland. Finally the city agreed to support the Prince in the States of Holland.

The First Stadhouderless period 1650-1672

However, much to the relief of many, William died suddenly at the end of 1650. There was no immediate heir as his only son was born nine days after his death. This confronted the young Republic with a new situation. A 'Grand Assembly' was convened at The Hague to deliberate on future policy; to it, each of the provinces sent a large group of representatives. The issues were 'Unity, the army and religion', with the provinces stressing the need that their full sovereignty on each issue be respected. To ensure their own power, they decided not to appoint a new Stadhouder for the time being.

The Navigation Act. The first 'English' or Anglo-Dutch war

Meanwhile, the continuing economic success of the Republic since the 1580's increased jealousy abroad, particularly in England. There, a Navigation Act was passed in 1651 for the protection of English shipping and trade. It ruled that European goods were only to be imported to England by English ships or by ships from the country of origin. Coastal trading with England was out of bounds to foreign shipping from then on.
This English intervention in the international free-trade system promoted by the Republic and aimed at one of the main elements in Dutch commercial success, the freight trade, led directly to the first Anglo-Dutch war (1652-1654). It was a bad war for the Republic. After the 'Three-Day Battle' at sea the English ruled the waves, even blockading the coast of Holland.
At the peace negotiations, representatives of the English Lord Protector, Oliver Cromwell, demanded guarantees from the Republic that the House of Orange would never be reinstated in its titles, showing his fear that the Oranges would support the restoration of a Stuart monarchy. The States-

General and the States of Holland again held opposing views on this point and this time Holland came off best. A few weeks after the Peace of Westminster was signed in 1654, Holland decided that no Prince of Orange would ever be appointed Stadhouder or Admiral of the province again. They would also oppose the appointment of an Orange to the position of Captain-General of the union by the States-General. This was known as the Act of Seclusion; secretly, it had already been included in the peace treaty with England. The plan had been devised by Pensionary John de Witt of Holland, from the powerful town of Dordrecht, who had been in charge of the politics of Holland since 1653; originally, his ideas on this and other points met with opposition from the other provinces, but his marriage to the daughter of one of Amsterdam's leading regents brought this influential city into his camp, strengthening his position.

Stadhouder William III

When the Stuarts returned to the throne of England in 1660, the position of the Oranges in the Republic was reinforced, and the Act of Seclusion revoked, partly due to pressure by the new English King Charles II, a cousin of young William III. For obvious political reasons, the States of Holland softened its anti-Orange attitude and offered to undertake the education of the prince, now ten years old. In 1666 he became a 'ward of state', a pupil of the States of Holland, because John de Witt wanted to restrict the influence of his maternal relatives, the Stuarts, on his upbringing to a minimum if only because, by that time, the Republic again was at war with England which in 1664 had taken New Amsterdam from the West India Company.
This second Anglo-Dutch war ended in a resounding success for the Dutch fleet under Admiral Michiel de Ruyter. It

Portraits of Prince William III of Orange and his wife Mary Stuart as King and Queen of England

destroyed a large part of the English fleet during a raid on the Medway in England and even captured the flagship 'Royal Charles' as booty. This victory at sea was largely due to the efforts of John de Witt in maintaining a strong, well equipped fleet. It helped much to tone down the terms of the Navigation Act in the ensuing peace treaty.

Grand Pensionary John de Witt

It had happened before that a Pensionary fell victim to the ambition and drive of a Prince of Orange. The same fate lay in store for John de Witt. He had done his best to build up the fleet, but he had neglected the army. The danger of this policy became apparent in 1672 when French intrigue prompted England and the independent Catholic principalities of Münster and Cologne to join France and declare war on the Republic – all within one month; soon, the entire south-eastern region of the Netherlands was occupied by the enemy. The people and some of the regents felt the need for a military man capable of inspiring confidence to the population; they now turned to the Prince of Orange; within two months he was appointed Stadhouder in all the provinces, except Friesland where members of the collateral branch of the Orange family had been holding this post since the late sixteenth century. William was also proclaimed Captain-General and Admiral-General.

The Pensionary had already admitted defeat by resigning his post when the French invaded, but he and his brother Cornelis now were lynched and killed by a furious

The murder of Johan and Cornelis de Witt, 20 August 1672. Engraving by Romeyn de Hooghe, 1672

mob in The Hague. The ringleaders were not punished for this shameful deed; on the contrary, they were rewarded by the Prince.

The struggle for a balance of power in Europe

As soon as he was appointed Captain-General, William III began to reorganize the neglected Dutch army. Admiral De Ruyter's victories at sea forced England to come to terms with the Dutch in 1674; William's own military successes led to peace with Münster and Cologne, leaving France the sole enemy. To some, the war which continued to be waged until 1678 increasingly seemed like a matter of personal and dynastic prestige in which, according to Williams critics the interests of the Republic took second place. However, to William it was a war that had to be waged and won in order to create a balance of power in Europe, to prevent France from achieving supreme hegemony; only thus could he secure continued independence for the Dutch. This concept was modern to the extent that it became a determining feature in many of the Republic's subsequent wars.

As in 1648 the regents soon could see no point in prolonging a costly war that damaged their commercial interests in France; they urged the Prince to come to terms with King Louis XIV. To the fury and disappointment of the Prince the Treaty of Nijmegen was negotiated in 1678.

However, William III eventually succeeded in reconciling the Republic to his grand strategy to achieve a balance of power. His marriage to another Mary Stuart, the daughter of James II of England, enabled him to become King of England in 1689 after his father-in-law had left the country in a state of political and religious turmoil. He then achieved his great wish of a Grand Alliance against France in which England, the Republic, the German Emperor, Spain and some of the German principalities were united. Meanwhile, Louis XIV had taken the side of James II in his attempt to regain the throne, but his main aim was to conquer both the Spanish Netherlands and the Republic itself. This marked the outbreak of a Nine Years' War between France and the anti-French coalition.
William decided that the Dutch should provide most of the resources for the war on land, while the English were to take the lead at sea. In so doing he unwittingly created a situation in which the maritime supremacy of the English both in war and in peace grew ever stronger; it caused the Republic to loose its erstwhile leading position in world trade.
For a long time, France was the strongest in combat on land, but at sea she was no match for the combined English and Dutch fleets. The war dragged on without a final victory for either side until France's interest in the War of the Spanish Succession took precedence over her wish to possess the Southern Netherlands. The Peace of Rijswijk was signed in 1697, allowing the Republic to garrison a number of fortresses towns in the Southern Netherlands, as a barrier against the inimical French.

Michiel de Ruyter (1607-1676), one of the Netherlands' most renowned admirals ▶

Family group portrayed in an 18th-century interior. The portrait between the windows honours a deceased member of the family. By H. Pothoven (Amsterdams Historisch Museum)

Society, politics and the economy in the late seventeenth and the eighteenth centuries

Although the seventeenth and eighteenth centuries have long been described as two contrasting periods in Dutch history, many eighteenth-century developments originated in the second half of the preceding century. Moreover, the alleged sudden decline of the Dutch Republic on all fronts of the economy and of culture is a fable. It was more of a gradual change in the economic and social climate, from vigorous and progressive to conservative. The need to make itself felt in the arena of European politics was satisfied once the Republic had found its niche among the other states. The wish to preserve the status quo now became stronger. Yet, the Dutch Republic continued to play an important part in world trade and through its investments retained its major hold over international finance. But even though there was no noticeable overall decline, competition from other countries, notably England and France, now prevented the country to hold on to the near-monopoly it had had for nearly a century.

Progress and decline

In the early part of the seventeenth century many wealthy merchants had invested in imaginative and even grandiose projects involving trade, industry and agriculture. The reclamation of land in North Holland for dairy farming was financed mainly from trade profits. In this way one enterprise led to the next. But in the eighteenth century investments were more often made abroad, especially in England and the Americas. Dutch international trade did not decline noticeably until fairly late in the eighteenth-century, but industry began to dwindle earlier. Partly as a result of the high wages paid here, production in, for example, the textile industry at Leiden dropped by 80% between 1670 and 1795. Shipbuilding too, which had flourished in the Golden Age, was now in recession.
Declining investment in domestic enterprises and the relatively generous wages customary in the Republic resulted in a high level of structural unemployment and poverty among the industrial part of the population. As the small group of wealthy investors grew wealthier, the social contrasts became greater than in the preceding centuries.

The regents and state government until 1747

Another cause of the widening gap between social groups was the concentration of power in the hands of a few leading families, both in the towns and in the country. There had been city oligarchies in the seventeenth century, but it had still been possible for new families to join the circle of regents, while others disappeared. In the eighteenth century such upward mobility became almost impossible; in almost all the cities most of the positions, from the highest to the most humble were actually controlled by a few regent families. They drew up mutual agreements, so-called 'contracts of correspondence', promising not to appoint anyone from outside their circle to any post. Agreements of this kind led to the appointment of newly-born babies to offices which were filled by substitutes who were paid a fraction of the actual salary. This form of nepotism and patronage bred corruption; it also caused dissatisfaction among the non-governing elite, the well-educated, wealthy patricians and bourgeois men who did not belong to the hallowed circle but felt they had every right to aspire to positions of power.

The increasing conservatism of the regents also influenced foreign policy. During the

War of the Spanish Succession (1702-1713) , Grand Pensionary Anthony Heinsius of Holland carried on the policy of William III to curb the power of France. But once the Treaty of Utrecht had been signed in 1713, many felt there was no further incentive to actively take part in foreign affairs. In this way the Republic lost prestige and failed to play a significant role on the international stage.

Part of the reason for this indifference to foreign affairs was the fact that by the time the Treaty of Utrecht was signed, the treasury was almost exhausted; moreover, the public debt, especially of Holland, had risen to such gigantic proportions that the economy was seriously affected. It was necessary to improve matters, among other things in the field of taxation, which had become a chaos. Adolf Hendrik, Count of Rechteren, called for a Grand Assembly to be held at The Hague in 1716, for the second time in the history of the Republic. At this meeting the secretary to the Council of State, Simon van Slingelandt, who was responsible for running the Union, proposed radical governmental reforms. The highly complex system of decision making, by which the delegates of the seven sovereign provinces had to consult their colleagues at home on every proposal put forward in the States-General, led to endless delays. But as the delegates at the Grand Assembly were subject to the same consultations, no agreement was reached and everything continued as before.

The Second Stadhouderless period 1702-1747

When William III died in 1702, it looked for a while as though the House of Orange had no further part to play, as he had been the last direct male descendant of William the Silent. The title of Prince of Orange passed to the Frisian line of the Nassau family. But John William Friso of Nassau, Stadhouder of Friesland and Groningen, was drowned in 1711. His widow, Maria Louise van Hessen-Kassel governed for their son William Charles Henry Friso, who had been born posthumously. She won widespread respect so that, when William came of age, he was able to take his place as Stadhouder in these two provinces without opposition. Gelderland also accepted him. The remaining provinces, led by Holland, chose to continue this second Stadhouderless period. William's marriage in 1734 to Anne, daughter of the new Hanoverian king of England, illustrates the importance still accorded to the title and status of Stadhouder abroad.

It was not until 1747, when the Republic became involved in the war of the Austrian Succession and invasion by French troops was imminent that, just as in 1672, the then Prince of Orange, William IV, was invited to become stadhouder in Holland, Zeeland, Utrecht and Overijssel. The Republic was involved in this war as a result of the Treaty of Vienna signed in 1731. This treaty between Austria, England, Spain and the Republic had important political and economic aspects. The countries involved acknowledged the right of Maria Theresia, daughter of the Austrian Emperor, to the succession in the lands under his rule. Since the Treaty of Utrecht of 1713 these included the Southern Netherlands. Now, for its involvement in this treaty, the Republic did ask a price; the Ostend Company, established in the Southern Netherlands in 1722, was dissolved as it had become a threat to the Dutch East India Company.
When Maria Theresia claimed her rights on the death of her father in 1746, other pretenders appeared on the scene. In the European war which followed the Republic was bound by the treaty to furnish troops, but it waited so long before doing so that it lost respect. Moreover, the King of France declared war on the Republic, England and Austria in 1744 and French troops invaded the Southern Netherlands, also capturing some of the fortressed barrier towns. By

1746 the South was almost entirely in the hands of the French; the Dutch part of Flanders was occupied in 1747.

The House of Orange: William IV and William V hereditary Stadhouders in all provinces

In 1747, the threat of war and the dissatisfaction with the rule of an ever more closed regent oligarchy that had been mounting over the preceding decades led to more or less spontaneous popular movements in many of the towns – some of them orchestrated by the partisans of the Prince -, asking for the recognition of William IV as hereditary Stadhouder in all provinces. Encouraged by this, wealthy non-regent burghers took the opportunity of seizing power by joining the cause of the House of Orange. They were Orangists for political reasons, only; as they regarded themselves as loyal to the 'fatherland', they have gained historical recognition as 'Patriots'.
In the following year the Treaty of Aix-la-Chapelle marked the end of the war. The Prince, safely installed in all provinces, was now free to deal with the many forms of corruption in the administration of the Republic. He was authorized to appoint regents at the local, regional and national level. But instead of doing away with the abuses of the former period, the Prince took the opportunity of appointing his devotees everywhere. This was a bitter disappointment to many of his supporters, who felt cheated in their own interests or realized that the reforms necessary to uphold the state were not forthcoming.
In Amsterdam, there was serious rioting in 1748 when the 'Doelisten', so-called after

18th-century view of Palace Het Loo at Apeldoorn,in a water-colour painting by Jan de Beijer. The carriage of Prince William IV is seen approaching the forecourt

18th-century painting by T.P.C. Haag portraying Prince William V – in scarlet coat with golden star – welcoming the Civic Guard in the gardens of Het Loo

the hall where they used to meet, voiced their demands. These included openness in appointments to public office, restoration of the privileges of the guilds and the allocation of the high proceeds from the postal service to the town. William IV came to Amsterdam in person and agreed to the demands.
But it was not long before things went on as before which led to a growing tendency among many educated non-regent burghers to unite in groups which voiced ever more radical ideas, even though these did not include any reference to such things as sovereignty for the people on the basis of general suffrage. A new political group emerged from this, a party almost, formed by the old regent aristocracy which had fallen from grace in 1747, and members of the wealthy bourgeoisie who still had no say in politics. Though they had different aims, they shared their dissatisfaction with the Stadhouder's administration which was stronger than ever before. This party also called itself Patriotic, but it differed from its predecessors of 1747 in that it was anti-Orangist. Their main aim was the constitutional reform of the decayed administrative system.
On the death of William IV in 1751, his

widow governed during the minority of their son William V, with the Duke of Brunswick acting as Captain-General. He was an Austrian field marshal, who had been engaged in the previous year to build up the Republic's army and had gained great influence with the Orange family.
The following years saw a bitter struggle between Amsterdam and William V, now of age, to decide whether to spend tax money on the equipment of the army or on the build-up of the fleet. As usual the Prince of Orange favoured the army which would strengthen his own position, while commercial Amsterdam was for the fleet. It was only in 1777, when England went to war against her American colonies, that the Republic finally decided to equip twenty men-of-war.
The support then given to the American rebels by the more democratic Dutch did not improve relations between the Republic and England. The decision of the States-General to provide convoys for the protection of the merchant fleet made matters worse. In December 1780, the fourth Anglo-Dutch War broke out during which Dutch maritime trade was very seriously damaged by the superior English navy.

Patriots and Orangists

The political differences between Patriots and Orangists now emerged clearly, as the Patriots blamed the Prince for this disaster because he, or at least his counsellors had always opposed enlarging the fleet.
In 1781, an anonymous pamphlet was distributed describing Patriot ideology. It was headed 'To the people of the Netherlands' and written by John Derk van der Capellen tot den Poll, a nobleman of Overijssel. He asked for reform but also advocated the establishment of volunteer corps of armed civic guards which in the following years were duly mustered everywhere.
During this period a more articulate party politics developed; it was both more theoretically refined than anything heard before and, moreover, described the need for reform in terms not of provincial sovereignty, only, but as something that should affect the entire country. Patriots from all over the Republic now met to draw up a kind of party manifesto. Patriotic newspapers such as the 'Post of the Lower-Rhine' were instrumental in this. In 1784 it was this paper that exposed the existence of the 'Consultation Act', an agreement between the Duke of Brunswick and William V, signed in 1766 when the Prince had just come of age. In it the Prince assured the Duke that he was only answerable to himself for any advice he might give him in the future. When this was publicized the indignation it caused was exaggerated, but the Duke had to leave the country and the anti-Orange mood deepened.

The Patriot movement found further inspiration in the successful American struggle for independence. At a congress of volunteer corps it was decided that the Republic should also be governed by representative government. Some of the Patriots drafted a new constitution closely resembling the American Declaration of Independence; this created a historically interesting situation, in that many of the American politicians themselves had gained some of their inspiration from the republican theories and practices of the Netherlands in the late sixteenth and early seventeenth century.

The Province of Utrecht, always a Catholic stronghold, and, moreover, with a capital where the traditions of the guilds were still respected, now became the centre of the Patriot movement. However, when a democratic administration was formed in this province in 1786, the rift in the movement due to the different backgrounds of the Patriots became apparent. The regents dismissed in 1747 were only in favour of abolishing the system of patronage in appointments as applied by the House of Orange

since then. But they would not agree to the far-reaching plans for reform drawn up by the burgher-Patriots.
With anti-Orange feeling deepening and the States of Holland, Zeeland, Groningen and Overijssel even suspending the Prince as Captain-General in 1786, the latter still remained popular with the general public. But, due to some unpolitical moves that further undermined his position, in 1787 he felt forced to call on his brother-in-law, the King of Prussia, to intervene on his behalf and reinstate him in his former power. This act of force was successful. The States of Holland were compelled to reverse all anti-Orange measures. But many Patriots fled to France, from where they continued the struggle with renewed vigour. They drew increasing sympathy, as William's reliance on foreign support and the way he tried to oust all political opponents in the following years was deeply resented in the Republic.

The arrest of Princess Wilhelmina near Goejanverwellesluis in 1787

Culture in the late seventeenth century and in the eighteenth century

Flowering and consolidation

Life in the Republic during the first half of the seventeenth century had been marked by flourishing activities in all fields of culture. The second half presents a more quiet image, as though it had lost some of its sparkle. Cultural activities began to move to the countryside as many wealthy merchants bought country houses, some with manorial rights and titles. Life in the country was idealized, especially in the literary work of the second half of the seventeenth century. In painting, idyllic landscapes were already popular in the 1640s; Jan Both (1618-1652) and Nicholaes Berchem (1620-1683) worked of this genre. At the same time, there was a general trend in favour of French culture among the upper classes. It was fashionable to speak French and French tastes in clothing and food were adopted. Of course, this wish for social distinction was due to the influence of the glittering court of King Louis XIV at Versailles. This court had become the cultural centre of Europe in the last decades of the seventeenth century; around c. 1700 its splendour came to influence culture in all the surrounding countries.

Architecture and interior decoration

After 1685, the arrival of numerous Huguenots, many of them able craftsmen and artists, also brought French styles of architecture, interior decoration and furnishings. Daniel Marot (1663-1752) was one of the newcomers; an engraver and interior decorator, he later worked as an architect. While he was employed at the court of William III, one of his designs was the interior of the Loo-palace, near Aperldoorn – the major remaining baroque structure of the Netherlands. Comprehensive designs for decorations and furnishings for entire interiors were new to the Republic and Marot and his followers created the trend. They also influenced the popular form of interior decoration practised in many parts of the country until well into the twentieth century. The beautifully painted interiors and furnishings of houses at Hindeloopen in Friesland and the Zaan in North Holland, were imitations of the style popular at court and in stately homes at the beginning of the eighteenth century. Marot also designed the Huguetan-mansion at The Hague. The delicate baroque style of this building was repeated by various other architects.
Later on in the eighteenth century, new styles of architecture and decoration were adopted. The architect Leendert Viervant designed a country house known as 'the Pavilion' for the wealthy banker and art-collector Henry Hope in Haarlem, in neo-classical style.

Painting

Painting suffered most from the widening gap between the different social groups. At the beginning of the seventeenth century art, at least partly, still reflected the life of ordinary people, which served as a colourful source of inspiration for genre painting. But this kind of work was not in demand with the people who bought or commissioned paintings in the eighteenth century. Bourgeois complacency looks out at us from the eighteenth century paintings by Wijbrand Hendriks (1744-1831), Adrian de Lelie (1755-1820) and John Ekels (1759-1793), the only high-light being the work of Cornelis Troost (1697-1750).
Painting was also influenced by French taste in interior decoration; walls were covered with decorative stucco and painted wallpaper leaving little space for individual paint-

The bedroom of Princess Mary, wife of Prince William III, in Het Loo. Decorations on the walls and the bed were restored to the original designs by Daniel Marot

Example of interior decoration at Hindeloopen – a Frisian village; folk art based on 18th-century aristocratic interior designs

ings. As a result, the art of painting wallpaper flourished in the second half of the eighteenth century. It was fashionable to depict arcadian scenes of refined pastoral life. Unfortunately most of this work has disappeared over the years as fashions changed again.

Literature

Wealthy burghers, rather more than patrons from the regent group, now set the trend in promoting literature. An example is the foundation of the 'Society for Dutch Literature' at Leiden in 1766. The members held monthly meetings, published their own works and maintained their own library. At first, French taste also prevailed in literature and the resulting work was not outstanding. However, many more people now became avid readers, aided by the number of journals of a general cultural nature produced in the Republic; though these mostly were written in French, they did help to spread the results of literary and scientific research and other cultural endeavours among a larger audience.
By the last decades of the century, the tentative beginnings of a new style appeared, less French-oriented both stylistically and as to its contents. The facts about Dutch middle-class society were revealed in light satirical vein, especially in the work of the ladies Elisabeth Wolff (1738-1804) and Agatha Deken (1741-1804). After her husband died, Mrs Wolff lived with her friend in the village of De Rijp. Together, they wrote several epistolary novels, following the example of the English author Samuel Richardson. The best-known of these is 'Sara Burgerhart' which appeared in 1782.
Another author looking for renewal at the end of the eighteenth century was the Pensionary of Leiden, Hieronymus van Alphen (1746-1803). To the general public, he is perhaps best known for his childrens' verse, which opens up a window to changing ideas about marriage and family life, as well as to didactic and pedagogical ideas. However, he was a versatile writer and influential cultural journalist as well who also published an introduction to new aesthetics.

Elisabeth Becker (1738-1804) and Agatha Deken (1741-1804), joint authors of the famous epistolary novel 'Sara Burgerhart'

Science and religion

In addition to the increased interest which they took in the fine arts, educated Dutch burghers also stimulated the exact sciences. These wide interests were in keeping with the rationalistic outlook on life which had been growing since the late seventeenth century. Natural science was the particular centre of attention, the more so as it promised spectacular technological improvements. The 'Dutch Society for Science' was founded at Haarlem in 1752 to stimulate scientific research. It held competitions asking for essays on a variety of scientific and other subjects, often setting specific problems which, if solved, could lead to industrial application or other practical results. Similar societies were formed in other towns; the members who stemmed from regent and well-to-do burgher circles alike, joined together in reading and commenting on scientific books watching physical experiments or even performing them themselves. Rationalistic thinking was also applied to religious matters. The French Encyclopedists while believing that the world was created by a God, held that it had afterwards developed along independent lines; there was a great deal of support for this view in Dutch educated circles, leading to all kinds of religious speculation and, though not widely, to a new spirit of free thinking that came to question traditional authority both in Church and in State.

Herman Boerhaave (1668-1738)

Society and politics (1787-1815); revolt and foreign rule

By the end of the eighteenth century, inflexibility and conservatism had penetrated so many aspects of life in the governing elite of the Republic that they were bound to awaken a new fighting spirit eventually. The gap between the well-to-do burghers and the lower classes mentioned above was one of the main problems. The dissatisfaction of many educated people with the ruling elite was another. But while the revolutionary spirit based on rationalistic ideas that appeared in North America and France at the end of the eighteenth century was alive in the Republic, too, the dissatisfied elements lacked the solidarity to bring about a revolution. The mob which was instrumental in bringing the revolution in France to its first successes, was mainly Orangeist in the Republic.

The Batavian Republic 1795-1806

In 1787, the revolt against the power of the Stadhouder had been crushed for the time being. In the following year, all the regents had to swear allegiance to the existing constitution and the provinces agreed mutually to safeguard the position of Stadhouder. When as a consequence of revolutionary developments in France, French troops invaded and occupied a large part of the Republic in 1795, this was partly at the instigation of the Patriots who had fled to France in 1787; the French soldiers hoped to strengthen the revolution against its foreign enemies, among which they counted the Orangeist Dutch Republic. Dutchmen in favour of reform now took the opportunity of seizing power, headed by Rutger Jan Schimmelpenninck (1761-1825). The Batavian Republic was proclaimed and Stadhouder William V fled to England, never to return.
Constitutional reforms were soon carried out, some of them modelled on the new French system. Elections were held for a National Assembly to replace the States-General. All male members of the population over the age of 20 and of fixed abode were eligible to vote if they were not living on charity. Another condition was that they had to forswear the Stadholderate.
The first meeting of the National Assembly was held on 1 March 1796. Soon, a committee was formed to draft a new constitution. But the Assembly proved to be divided by a bitter controversy between federalists, who were in favour of maintaining provincial independence, and unitarians, who were against it and wanted a centralised state.
After much bickering a constitution based on unitarian principles was adopted in April 1798 which divided the country into eight departments. Local and departmental authorities were to be elected by those eligible to vote. The same applied to the Legislative Assembly, a national body with the power to appoint an Executive Council of five directors.

The new constitution became effective during the same year. The system that for two hundred years had been the Republic of the Seven United Dutch Provinces ceased to exist. The new order soon materialised. In 1798, a separation between State and Church was effectuated, which opened the way to the legal equality of all denominations and religions; especially the Roman Catholics and the Jews were now given the possibility to once more worship in public. Gradually, a number of fiscal and legal measures, and the parallel centralization of government paved the way for further progress towards national unity. Still, the new Dutch state functioned under French supervision, only.

Scheveningen 1795: the departure of Prince William V for England

In 1801 a coup was staged by the French commander, General Augereau with the help of three members of the Executive Council, to bring the Republic even more into line with France's anti-English policy. A new constitution was implemented which on some points recreated the situation that had existed before 1795.
In 1805 there were consultations between Napoleon, the French dictator turned emperor, and Rutger Jan Schimmelpenninck, the Netherlands' envoy in Paris. Napoleon now favoured the introduction of monocratic rule hoping this would improve the organization of Dutch support in the French struggle against England. Schimmelpenninck returned to the Netherlands to present the voters with a draft constitution granting executive power to a new official, typically to be called Pensionary: people still thought in terms reminiscent of the Dutch old regime. He himself would be the first to hold this office. There was also to be a Legislative Assembly of 19 members authorized to appoint the Pensionary and with the right to vote bills. Schimmelpenninck could count on the help of several able ministers and with them he pursued a fairly progressive policy. National regulations for elementary education were provided for the first time in the Education Act of 1806. Responsibility for education

Louis Napoleon Bonaparte (1778-1846),
King of Holland from 1806 until 1810

now lay with the state instead of the town councils, the Church or with private schools. Teacher-training was instituted as well to guarantee a certain quality of education. Unfortunately Schimmelpenninck had to resign his office after only a year when, in 1806, Napoleon proclaimed the Batavian Republic a part of the French Empire, and, moreover, a kingdom, with his youngest brother Louis Napoleon as its initially unwilling king.

Meanwhile, the economy of the Netherlands had declined steadily since 1795. Overseas trading came to a standstill. During the last quarter of the eighteenth century, the Dutch East India Company had suffered such heavy losses that it had to be liquidated. In 1798, the Batavian Republic took over its debts and assets, and on 31 December 1799 this renowned and once so successful trading company ceased to exist. The West India Company had already been disbanded in 1791.

When France imposed the so-called 'continental system' on all its dependent states to block commerce with England, overseas trade became virtually impossible; this was a disaster for a country that practically thrived on it. Moreover, the alliance of the former Republic, now the Kingdom, with France involved it ever closely in the French wars with England, which now saw its chance to occupy the Dutch colonies, one by one. Most of these overseas territories were only returned in 1814, at the London Convention.

Dutch industry, too, was in a poor state. Small-scale business accounted for most of the production. There was no question as yet of technical innovations such as those introduced in the Flemish textile industry. Business initiatives by wealthy burghers were not to be expected, especially as they had been forced to accept a severe loss on their investments when the national debt was reduced to a third after the annexation by France.

The Kingdom of Holland under Louis Napoleon 1806-1810

Though the new king had accepted his throne only reluctantly, he soon grew to actually love his new kingdom, or perhaps rather his new role, to the extent that his imperial brother became wary of his enthusiasm. Indeed, Louis's government certainly was not unbeneficial to the Netherlands. On a great number of counts, it pursued the centralizing, rational policy adopted in the preceding years, and gave it new stimuli, as in the improvement of infrastructure.

Of undeniable importance was the introduction, in 1808, of a new civil code on French lines, which greatly influenced life in all its legal aspects, the more so as precisely in this respect the seven republics had been hopelessly divided. In 1810, the system of communal registry offices was adopted for the compulsory registration of births, deaths and marriages – which, of course, was of no mean help to the government's fiscal-economic policies. Many Dutch families now were given a name for the first time.

Louis Napoleon encouraged a number of important cultural developments. In 1808, the Royal Institute for Science, Literature and the Arts was founded at his instigation. One of its tasks was to organize an exhibition of work by contemporary Dutch artists, to be held every other year; this certainly encouraged the arts in various ways.

Louis Napoleon also paved the way for the 'Rijksmuseum' of later date. He started a Royal Museum in part of the old Town Hall of Amsterdam which he had had converted for use as a Royal Palace. Although most of the works which he kept there came from the former Stadhouder's collection, the King took great pleasure in royally adding to it. For instance, he included Rembrandt's 'Night Watch' which still belonged to the city of Amsterdam, although it was not at all in popular taste at the time. In creating the Museum, Louis gave the Netherlands a temple to glorify their national memories in, enabling the Dutch to identify with their great past.

In 1809, Louis Napoleon's reign was cut short by the unsuccessful English invasion of Zeeland. He even attempted to defend the country entrusted to him against an army sent by his brother, the Emperor, but the Dutch, quite surprisingly, did not dare to support him. In 1810, he abdicated in favour of his small son, who never became king of the Netherlands, but, eventually, did become the Emperor Napoleon III of France.

The Netherlands annexed by and opposed to France 1810-1813

By this time Emperor Napoleon had already decided to annexe the Netherlands to France, to realize an old ambition viz. the possession of the Rhine Delta.
Conscription to military service, determined by lot, was introduced in 1811 to bring Napoleon's army up to strength. As a result, nearly 15,000 Dutch soldiers were forced to accompany Napoleon on his ill-fated Russian campaign in the following year. Very few of them survived this terrible experience. This, and the economic recession which set in when the Netherlands was forbidden to trade with England or non-European countries, caused anti-French feeling to run high. As always in a crisis, the people turned to the House of Orange once more. The defeat of Napoleon by a European coalition at Leipzig in 1813, signalled the retreat of French troops from Dutch soil. Three Orangist regents, Van Hogendorp, Van der Duyn van Maasdam and Van Limburg Stirum took power and governed the land awaiting the return of the Orange-family.

Three Orangist regents, Van Hogendorp, Van der Duyn van Maasdam and Van Limburg Stirum took power and governed the land awaiting for the return of the Orange-family.

King William I, his two sons, his wife and his daughter, on the occasion of his inauguration, painted by J.L. Goudband

Society, politics, economy and culture in the Kingdom of the United Netherlands 1815-1830/1839

Reunion of the Northern and Southern Netherlands: the constitution of 1815

At the invitation of the three interim governors, the heir to the House of Orange landed at Scheveningen on 30 November 1813. He was the son of the last Stadhouder, William V, who had died in exile. The prince was inaugurated as the sovereign ruler, King William I (1772-1843) at Amsterdam on 2 December. In 1814 he also accepted sovereignty over the Southern Netherlands. In 1815, he proclaimed himself 'King of the Netherlands', thus reuniting the seventeen provinces of the Northern and Southern Netherlands after a separation of over 225 years.

Portrait of King William I by J.B. van de Hulst (Amsterdams Historisch Museum)

But the reunion was not destined to last. Differences in economics, religion, culture and politics had grown too great. One might even question whether the cohesion often claimed by the adherents of the so-called 'greater Netherlands' idea' ever was a historical reality. The seventeen Netherlands actually only functioned in a personal union under Charles V for a few decades in the sixteenth century. And during the two centuries of the Republic even the seven sovereign states had had serious problems in accepting their own differences.

One of the points of friction in the new kingdom was the composition of the Lower House. In the South, the population was bigger than in the North, and yet each part was represented in it with 55 members, with meetings held alternately at The Hague and Brussels. Soon the Southern members, representing a mainly Roman Catholic population, complained of strong discrimination against them and began to sabotage many government proposals. This caused the King to rule by Royal Decree, mostly, which itself raised more opposition, now also from liberals in both North and South. In 1828, this even resulted in an 'unholy alliance' between Southern Catholics and the liberals, who proposed to co-operate in eliminating the existing problems.

One of the major difficulties was denominational education, more specifically as provided by the religious orders, as it required permission from the state. As education in the South had always been the province of the Roman Catholic Church, this measure was felt to be intolerably patronizing. Language was another problem. William I decreed that the civil service was to use

Dutch, in an effort to speed up the unification of the two halves of the kingdom into one, national culture. But both in the Walloon provinces, and in the upper classes of Flanders, French was normally spoken. This accentuated existing socio-economic differences and power positions but was unacceptable in the new 'national' vision.
Press censorship, too, caused trouble. People were taken to court for insulting the government or even for voicing critical remarks about government policy; this added to the strain on the relations between William I and his Southern subjects.
When an industrial crisis threatened in 1830, with the Southerners blaming the government for a free trade policy in which their industrial products were not protected in any way while Northern commerce was unduly favoured, all the ingredients of rebellion were present, the more so as foreign influences – French ones among them – worked against William's position.

The establishment of the Belgian State: 1 October 1830

After some rioting and disturbances in Brussels and other places in the South, a temporary administration was set up by dissatisfied Southerners in September 1830. An independent state called Belgium was proclaimed on 1 October and a national conference was convened.
In November the foreign powers interested in the status of the Netherlands, including Russia, England, France, Prussia and Austria met in London. Especially England, that had been building its own position as a leading industrial nation in these decades, realized that it did not exactly favour a territorially and economically competitive 'greater' Netherlands, while the French had not yet lost their perennial aversion against a strong power on their northern borders. A month later, the Kingdom of the Netherlands had been dissolved and in January 1831 the separation of Belgium was formalized.
While the King was prepared to accept the decisions of the London Conference, the Belgians felt slighted by some of the clauses. A later proposal made in June was acceptable to the Belgians, but not to the King. Meanwhile, Leopold of Saxe-Coburg had been elected King of the Belgians.
William I persisted in refusing the new proposals. In August the notorious Ten-Day Campaign took place, during which the Dutch army initially defeated the Belgians, but was forced to retreat when the French intervened.

A truce was finally concluded in 1833, but it was not until 1838 that William I agreed to the clauses drawn up at the London Conference. The final treaty, acceptable to all parties, was signed in 1839; it marked the end of the brief reunion of the Southern and Northern Netherlands. Since then the North has been known as the Kingdom of the Netherlands.

William I, the Merchant-King: trade and industry

Though William I met with increasing resistance from parts of the population because of his high-handed behaviour, his contribution to economic revival in both North and South was tremendous. He earned his nickname of 'merchant-king' by his tireless efforts to restore prosperity to the Netherlands' trade and industry. One of his initiatives was to set up the Dutch Trading Company. The King personally invested 4 million guilders in this company – some hundreds of millions in present-day currency – and guaranteed the other shareholders a dividend of 4% for the first 25 years. He then proceeded to try and help the Company to conquer the developing markets of the newly-independent Latin American states, assuming, wrongly, that the Dutch would have easy access, there, due to their colonial past. After 1830 the activities of this company were concentrated

on trade with the Netherlands East Indies. There, Governor-general John van den Bosch introduced the 'cultivation system'. Native farmers were forced to use a fifth of their land to produce the crops ordered by the government. The resulting products such as coffee and sugar were shipped to the Netherlands by the Dutch Trading Company and marketed both nationally and internationally. Return cargo consisted, among other things, of cotton clothing from Twente. In this way Dutch industry was supplied with raw materials and Dutch trade found an outlet.
For the cotton industry had been initiated in Twente in 1833 for the manufacture of goods mainly for the Indian market. Its success was partly due to the fact that by now the Belgian textile industry was no competitor anymore.
There were other ways in which William I tried to stimulate the economy. The Bank of the Netherlands and the State Mint were established on his instigation, to ensure control of the money market. The gradual introduction of the metric system, though not an easy operation, was meant to favour economic life as well. He also improved transportation by promoting road-building and repairs, and the construction of canals. The North Holland Canal connecting the capital with the open sea, re-opened the port of Amsterdam to large vessels. At the end of William's reign in 1839 the first of the Netherlands' railways was opened, between Amsterdam and Haarlem.
Private enterprise was also instrumental in making the Netherlands a great trading power once more. The Steamship Companies of Rotterdam and Amsterdam were founded in 1823 and 1825 respectively, and together they built up the modern shipbuilding industry.

Though the economy was gradually recovering, there was widespread poverty in the first decades of the nineteenth century. The so-called 'Relief Company' was founded in 1818 to combat this by providing employment for those who had not been able to earn a living before. The development of waste land was undertaken in Drenthe, in preparation for agriculture and cattle breeding.
The reclamation of one of the last remaining lakes, the Haarlemmermeer, also created a large stretch of new land. At this time, plans were even made for the reclamation of the Zuiderzee. Of course, these measures could not structurally eradicate poverty.

Consequently, many of those dependent on, especially, agriculture decided to leave home and seek their fortunes abroad. In the course of the nineteenth century the United States of America, with its promise of unlimited possibilities became their new fatherland; still, many emigrants continued to cling to their own culture for generations, specifically through their own schools and newspapers.

Culture and religion under William I

It was William's policy to promote the Dutch language for the good of creating a common culture. Nevertheless, regional dialects, sometimes with a high degree of linguistic independence, survived; and, consequently, regional cultures survived, especially in the more rural areas, where the culture of the new, urban, industrial elite could not penetrate to do its unifying job. In painting, too, this quest for national symbols was reflected. So-called historical painting flourished, with subjects from the history of the Netherlands in the sixteenth and seventeenth centuries as favourite topics. Undeniably, it was during the nineteenth century that this earlier period took on its image of a 'Golden Age' on which the Dutch looked back with justifiable pride.
William's educational policy, though a problem in his relations with the South, was not without effect, either. In Delft he established the Academy for Civil Engineering, to con-

tribute both to economic life and to the needs of the military. It was one of the centres from which a new use of mathematics was propagated to help solve the problems of man and society – an approach favoured by William's education ministers in other school types as well.

In the same spirit of building a national culture, William I wanted to turn the Dutch Reformed Church into a haven for every Dutchman. This was unacceptable to some dogmatically protestant movements, resulting in a schism in 1834. The government reacted so harshly that many of the followers of this puritan group, too, decided to emigrate to the U.S.A.
Meanwhile, though the law guaranteed freedom of religion, there was no real equality in this field as yet.

The King's abdication: 1840

After a controversial reign lasting 27 years, William I had alienated himself from the people by his self-willed policy, but he had worked wonders for the economy, promoting and developing prosperity in the land. However, in 1848 he was compelled to abdicate in favour of his son. His position had become intolerable when, after the death of his first wife, Frederica of Prussia, he announced his intention of marrying a Roman Catholic, the Belgian Countess Henrietta d'Oultremont. After his abdication he left for Berlin where he died in 1843.

Lithograph showing the Rijnspoorweg station at Utrecht, already one of the busiest railway junctions in the Netherlands during the second half of the 19th-century

Society, politics and economy: towards an industrial society. The first phase, until c. 1890

The constitutional revisions of 1840 and 1848

In 1840, as a result of the independence of Belgium constitutional revision was necessary. Some of the leading liberals as well as some progressive Roman Catholic leaders saw a chance of introducing a number of democratic reforms. Most important of these was the introduction of ministerial responsibility. This would enable parliament to call ministers to account for the policy pursued, where formerly they reported to the King alone. Realizing that this would greatly restrict his political power, the new King, William II (1840-1848) rejected the proposed reforms. He would only agree to the introduction of a limited form of ministerial responsibility, which held ministers accountable in case they acted against the law.
In the following years the government and the reformers were unable to reach an agreement. Only when he was faced with the threat of revolution – which became a reality in many European states in 1848 –

The great liberal politician J.R. Thorbecke (1798-1872), after a portrait by J.H. Neuman, c. 1852 (Rijksmuseum, Amsterdam)

the King came to accept a more rigorous constitutional revision. The new constitution was proclaimed on 3 November, as drafted by a committee of which the liberal leader John Rudolph Thorbecke (1798-1872) was a member.
The most important amendments concerned state administration. Ministerial responsibility to parliament was introduced, ensuring that, henceforth, the King could do no wrong. From now on, the members of the Upper Chamber of Parliament, instead of being appointed by the King, would be elected by the Provincial States. The Lower Chamber, as well as the Provincial States and municipal councils were to be elected directly by the electorate. The right to vote was, however, restricted to those men who paid taxes – general suffrage was not introduced, yet. The Lower Chamber was given the rights of amendment, interpellation and enquiry. Also, it was ruled that all meetings of representative bodies were to be held in public.

Limitation of the King's power

The constitutional revision of 1848 had reduced the political power of the King to a few well-defined rights. One of these was the right to dissolve Parliament. In practice this only applied to the Lower Chamber, with the odd exception.
King William II could not resign himself to these infringements. His son William III (1849-1890), too, had great difficulty in staying aloof from the parties and refrain from meddling in politics. In 1866, a clash of wills occurred when the King dissolved both Chambers because he was reluctant to accept the resignation of the government. He ordered new elections, and advised people to vote for a Parliament which would support the team he favoured. However, the King was not permitted to show such partisanship.
Still, at first he had his way, and the cabinet stayed on. But at the first opportunity the

The future King William II (1840-1849) as portrayed by J.A. van Tetroode in 1819

new Lower Chamber expressed its disapproval of government policy. Again, the government tendered its resignation, and again the King dissolved the Chamber. In the newly-elected Parliament, the liberals were strongly represented; the Lower Chamber now explicitly rejected the dissolution. The King then had to admit defeat and the cabinet was sent home.
A new cabinet led by the liberal Thorbecke took its place. Since then the Dutch rulers have, by and large, accepted their position as a symbol of the unity of the Dutch

people, although William III continued to find this irksome. When his daughter Wilhelmina, who had succeeded him in 1890 at the tender age of 10, actually took on her responsibilities, she, too, found it difficult to comply with the rules of the constitutional game. Actually exercising considerable influence behind the screens – as have done her daughter and granddaughter, she still was generally respected for the conscientious way she fulfilled her role. Especially the vigorous way in which she behaved during the Second World War earned her a reputation which, finally, ensured her the position of 'mother of the fatherland', which she has been accorded in Dutch historiography.

In the period between 1840 and 1914, the Netherlands developed from a predominantly agricultural society into an industrial one. In 1840, the year of William I's abdication, society was not yet on its way towards industrialization. True, the textile industry in Twente was flourishing, but there was no large-scale, heavy industry to speak of. Influenced by liberal ideas, in the following years, the Dutch economy gradually developed towards a modern, industrial-capitalist system. Especially prime minister Thorbecke did much to stimulate the transition from a mercantile to a free-trade policy. Yet, around the 1850s, in the field of technology and engineering the Netherlands still lagged behind most of the industrialized European nations. The expansion of the railway network proceeded only slowly. It was not until the 1860s, when government decided to intervene, that the construction of railways was speeded up.

Workers unite

Yet, industry gradually took the place of agriculture as the foremost means of support. In the second half of the century most of the manual work was taken over by machines. To factory workers, these developments were not beneficial. The liberal distaste of government intervention, as well as the reluctance on the entrepreneurs' part to invest in improved working conditions meant that there was hardly any protection of workers' rights. When times were bad, wages were low; working hours always were long; child labour was regarded as inevitable.
Gradually, a mood of protest grew against the inhuman conditions in which people were forced to live and work.
Initially, private initiative, such as displayed by the 'Society for the Common Wealth', tried to combat social problems; actions were undertaken in the field of alcoholism, which was widespread, in the field of the vocational education of girls and women, as yet poorly implemented, et cetera. In the course of the century, political groups such as the socialists undertook to help workers to speak out. Soon, the workers themselves decided to unite in an effort to achieve better working conditions. The Netherlands General Workers' Union was formed in 1872. It still was opposed to striking as a means to effectuate socio-economic change. This also applied to the Protestant Union, 'Patrimonium', founded in 1876, and to the 'Roman Catholic Workers' Union, formed by the priest Alphons Ariens.

But at the beginning of the twentieth century the argument over the right to strike was in full swing. The government attempted to stave off the possibility of a strike by passing laws prohibiting civil servants to use it as a form of protest. This led to a railway strike in 1903; a second one, which was meant to be a general strike, failed when it was called for. Many workers were still unsure of their rights in this respect.

The first social legislation

For all this, the first social law was not the work of socialists or organized workers. It was the liberal Member of Parliament

Samuel van Houten who, in 1874, introduced a bill prohibiting child labour for those who were under 12 years of age. Slowly, people began to realize that the inhuman circumstances in which many had to survive could no longer be tolerated. In 1886, the government ordered an inquiry into the condition of factory workers. Action did not follow immediately, but the inquiry itself was a sign of the changing attitude to social problems. As a result, a number of laws were passed in the following years which led to a general improvement in the position of workers. The Factory Act was passed in 1889 which prohibited child labour altogether and, moreover, regulated working conditions for adolescents and for women. A system of factory inspection was introduced to ensure that these regulations were observed.
However, only when general education became compulsory in 1900 a real stop was put to child labour.

Emancipation of Roman Catholics and Jews

The constitution of 1848 had recognized the right to freely worship one's religion. But the subsequent re-establishment of the bishoprics and, consequently, of the Catholic

A clothing factory in Amsterdam, depicted by H.J. Wolters (Amsterdams Historisch Museum)

hierarchy in 1853, after 250 years, brought furious protests from dogmatic Protestant circles; the reactions for and against, the so-called 'April Movement', shook the nation. Thorbecke's first cabinet fell on account of this affair. But emancipation of the Roman Catholics took place all the same, slowly but surely. By that time the Jews who, as a far smaller group, posed less of a threat to the ruling elite and the prevailing religious-cultural climate, had succeeded already in securing a better position.

Denominational and non-denominational education: the battle over the schools

The constitution of 1848 also had established people's right to choose their own system of education. This gave rise to a fierce struggle over financial equality of denominational education. Until now only non-denominational, 'neutral' education had been funded by the government. A 'battle over the schools' resulted in which both the Catholics and the Dutch Reformed communities began to tighten their organizations to enforce their right to have their own state-financed form of education and, hence, of culture. Legislation was eventually passed in 1889 granting that the government would also fund denominational education. However, full equality was not realized till the constitutional reform of 1917.

In 1863, Thorbecke also provided for a law on secondary education, resulting in the foundation of the so-called 'Higher Burgher School', or H.B.S. It was to replace the old-fashioned 'French Schools' and to provide training geared to a modern, industrial society. Like the Latin schools (known as Gymnasia since 1876), the Higher Burgher Schools were soon preparing students for a university education.
In this welter of socio-emancipatory movements, the women of the Netherlands could now be clearly heard for the first time, speaking up in defence of a fairer society in which they would no longer be regarded as second-rate citizens. Aletta Jacobs was an example to many; in 1870, she was the first girl to be admitted to the H.B.S., and she went on to complete her education at the university. She became the first woman physician in the Netherlands.

Ethical politics in relation to the colonies

The constitution of 1848 also was of great importance to the development of the Dutch colonies. Until then the King had ruled supreme in colonial affairs, being represented by a governor-general. But this power, too, was taken from him in 1848.

King William III (1849-1890)

Working the fields in colonial Java, from a series of paintings by W.O.J. Nieuwenkamp, made in 1927 for the boardroom of the Handelsvereniging Amsterdam (SNS Bank, Amsterdam)

This meant that a new form of government had to be set up in the Dutch East Indies. A new system also was introduced in the Antilles in 1865; and Surinam even was given an elected parliament.

Just as there was a heightened awareness of social abuse in the Netherlands themselves, among critics at home there was a growing realization that the colonies and their inhabitants were being exploited, too. In 1860, the writer Edward Douwes Dekker protested under the name of 'Multatuli' ('I have suffered greatly') against the excesses of forced cultivation in his famous novel: 'Max Havelaar, or the coffee auctions of the Dutch Trading Company'. The outcry it caused was not in vain. The cultivation system was abolished a decade later when the Cultivation Act was adopted. This enabled farmers to lease land from the Dutch government without the obligation of growing specific crops for the export market.

In 1899 a sensational article called 'A debt of honour' was published in an influential literary magazine called 'De Gids' (The Guide). It marked the beginning of the so-called ethical policy, favoured by those politicians who advocated a slow evolution to eventual self-rule for the colonies. But many years were to pass before this point was actually reached.

For a long time the Netherlands was in favour of maintaining slavery in its slave-driven plantation colony of Surinam. It means the Netherlands were a party in the international discussion over the abolition of the slave trade with Africa, and of slavery itself in the Americas; it has to be admitted that the Dutch held on to the system for a rather long time. Slavery was only abolished in 1863. Inevitably, the economy of Surinam fell into a recession, in spite of the arrival of Hindustani immigrants from British India, and of Javanese labourers from the Dutch East Indies – an immigration strongly stimulated by the Dutch government and, therefore, not to be considered entirely free. Its very fact, however, contributed to the establishment of a multi-cultural society in this West-Indian colony.

The political parties take shape

In the Netherlands, political parties in the modern sense began to form hesitantly around 1880, as a result of industrialization, social organization and the religious-political agitation surrounding legislation on schools. The Anti-Revolutionary Party had been founded in 1878, on the basis of a program provided by Abraham Kuyper. The liberals organized themselves in the Liberal Union in 1885, on a much less rigid footing. In 1883, the Roman Catholic leader Schaepman presented a political manifesto which however was not accepted by a majority of Catholic voters until 1896. The socialists had already entered the political arena in 1888, when the former Lutheran preacher Ferdinand Domela Nieuwenhuis became the first socialist to be elected to the Lower Chamber. Domela Nieuwenhuis, who had been in prison for lèse-majesté only a year before, was the leader of the Social-Democratic Union founded in 1881.

Pillarization

One of the consequences of the emancipatory movements of the later nineteenth century was the way in which the Netherlands became 'pillarized'. Dutch society came to consist of a number of sharply distinct groups, characterized by their own religious and political ideas, which also reflected themselves in the economic, social and cultural choices people made: in sports and in music, in literature and in the arts, and even in the media, people organized themselves according to the dictates of their 'pillar'. Power blocks were the result, with their own political parties, schools and professional organizations. Priests and ministers did not hesitate to use the pulpit to incite their faithful to strictly remain within these groups. A natural consequence was the call for general suffrage; for 'pillarization' had given the political leaders a definite following, that, if given the vote, could be used to effect the greatest good for its own group. Paradoxically, this turned Dutch parliamentary democracy into a definitely consensual system that could only work because the various groups or 'pillars' constantly looked for the coalition that would be most advantageous.

Prof. Dr. H. Schaepman who, in 1896, founded the Roman Catholic Party

A slave market in Surinam, c. 1830 ▶

Between 1848 and 1887, the number of men eligible to vote by law was still small. But in 1887 the constitution was revised once more, including an electoral reform whereby everyone who could prove financial well-being and moral decency was eligible to vote. Admittedly, voting was still reserved exclusively for men. In the eyes of socialists and radicals this reform did not go far enough; they were in favour of universal suffrage.

In 1896 the number of voters rose to more than half of the adult male population as a result of yet another electoral reform. But universal male suffrage was not adopted until 1917, and women had to wait for another two years.

Culture in the nineteenth century: a long-forgotten chapter

Till the 1970s, cultural development in the Netherlands during the nineteenth century usually was described as complacent, provincial and unoriginal. Nowadays people are willing to admit that there were many new developments, with a decided originality.

Painting: the 'School of The Hague' and Vincent van Gogh

After the flourishing of historical painting at the beginning of the nineteenth century, art in the Netherlands became more academic: inspiration seemed to be derived solely from traditional themes. But during the second half of the century, a number of artists specializing in marine paintings and in landscape began to produce work that resembled and, it has to be admitted, even preceded the work of the School of Barbizon and the Impressionists in France. From the 1870s, those who settled in or around The Hague were termed the 'School of The Hague'. Such men as John Weissenbruch and the internationally successful Anton Mauve belonged to this 'school'; important work was being done, too, by the brothers Jacob and Willem Maris. A third brother, Matthijs, produced paintings akin to the symbolists, a European movement which flourished briefly at the end of the nineteenth century. George Breitner painted in true impressionist vein. His street scenes of Amsterdam are particularly expressive.

This on the whole surprisingly vital artistic climate, that gave opportunities to many, was the background against which the genius of Vincent van Gogh (1853-1890) was unfolding. He, surely the best-known Dutch artist since Rembrandt, began working in Drenthe and Brabant, but produced his most famous paintings after he had moved to France, where the bright light of the Provence never ceased to inspire him.
The early work of Mondriaan has to be situated in this context as well; in his case, an impressionist vision developed along ever more expressionist lines towards an almost absolute abstraction.

Architecture: Cuypers and Berlage

After the 1850s, the restrained neo-classicism that had been fashionable for many decades was replaced by neo-gothic architecture, mainly prompted by the Roman Catholic emancipation. The major representative of this movement was the architect Pierre Cuypers, who restored and designed numerous Catholic churches all over the country. He also built the Amsterdam Central Station and the Rijksmuseum. This demonstrated that emancipation really was making progress: even such 'national' monuments were given a neo-gothic, and hence to many 'Catholic' appearance, despite the fact that critics did not hesitate to denounce this very aspect of these prestigious buildings.
Many architects rejected the return to overdecoration and to traditional models inherent in neo-gothic building; but precisely the tradition of craftsmanship that went with it, became a fertile soil from which grew the initiatives of new architects who truly renovated Dutch building. Hendrik Petrus Berlage was one such innovator. The new Amsterdam Exchange, and the castle of St. Hubert on the Hoge Veluwe reflected his idea that the interior structure of a building should be visible in its outward appearance, not glossed over with unnecessary decoration.

Literature and music: the 'Men of the Eighties' and the Socialists

As Dutch society became ever more industrialized, many people felt the need to escape from the anonymous, collectivist atmosphere which increasingly seemed to pervade life. That need was reflected in impressionist painting but also in literature. Many younger authors rebelled against what was denigratingly called the parson's poetry of the mid-nineteenth century. The literary movement of the 'Men of the Eighties' which included writers and poets such as Jacques Perk and Willem Kloos expressed an individualistic awareness of life, resulting in a late romantic, impressionist glorification of nature. At the same time other authors decided to use poetry and literary prose precisely to feature the problems of the new, industrial society, thus to attract attention to them; Herman Gorter and Henriette Roland Holst were among those who expressed their socialism in poetic lines.

Music first produced such interesting composers as J. van Bree, whose third symphony celebrated 'the fatherland', and J Verhulst, who in his many songs used Dutch lyrics instead of the ubiquitous German poetry. They were followed by the one truly great Dutch composer of the past two centuries, Alphons Diepenbrock (1862-1921). He wanted to give music a place again in society and culture, searching for a synthesis between old-Netherlandish forms, the new ideas put forward by Richard Wagner in the 1860s and 1870s and the aesthetic of the modern French composers who worked around the turn of the century.

Vincent van Gogh (1853-1890). A rest at noon

Society, politics and the economy: towards an industrial society. The second phase, c. 1890-1945

The development of a society cannot be confined between specific dates, but it is safe to state that the first phase of Dutch industrialization was completed during the last decades of the nineteenth century. In the following decades the Netherlands developed into one of the most highly-industrialized countries in the world, despite a lapse during the depression in the nineteentwenties and 'thirties.

The concept of neutrality

Already in the decade before the First World War actually broke out, the threat of war could be felt all over Europe. The Netherlands, too, took steps to defend itself in case of need and laws were passed in 1912 and 1913 to bring the army up to standard. However, the wish to remain neutral prevailed. General mobilization was ordered in August 1914, but this was only in order to prepare for a possible infringement of neutrality by Germany.

The Depression during the 'thirties'

The economic depression which had developed after the First World War, reached its crisis in the period after 1929. The liberal view that the government should not intervene in economic affairs had become untenable. A growing consciousness of social problems also demanded other measures than those which promoted prosperity, only. Working hours had been cut in 1922, already. During the Depression national assistance was given to the unemployed, guaranteeing them a minimum income, however small. When, in 1933, unemployment was exceptionally high, the Ministry of Social Affairs was formed. Unemployment peaked in 1935 with over 30% of the labour force out of work. Then, the so-called 'Plan for Labour' was put forward by the socialists, who strongly rejected liberal ideas on factory management. It advocated substantial government investment and a planned economy. By devaluating the guilder, the government succeeded in cutting unemployment figures slightly, but by 1939 there were still 300,000 people unemployed. Not surprisingly, during these difficult decades many people left the Netherlands once more; for most emigrants, the United States remained their favourite destination.

Poster announcing the 'Exhibition for Peace and the League of Nations' on the Binnenhof, The Hague, 1930

A mass demonstration held in The Hague in 1932 organized by the Socialist Party, demanding more jobs and welfare for all

Government policy during the Depression

The man who as prime minister left his mark on government policy in these years of crisis was Hendrik Colijn (1869-1944); he was prime minister five times between 1925 and 1939. He obstinately worked to maintain the gold standard, regarding the final devaluation of the guilder as a defeat. Though many agreed with him, he still won a great victory with his Anti-Revolutionary Party in the elections of 1937. In need of a strong figure, many non-Protestant voters wanted Colijn to return which enabled him to form his fourth cabinet.

The main remedy which Colijn had in mind to combat the Depression was to enforce drastic budget cuts. This view clashed with the socialist Plan for Labour. While Colijn did not steep up government investments, he did attempt to bring down unemployment figures by job-creation schemes. The major project in this field was the reclamation of the Zuiderzee. Plans to drain it had already been made in the nineteenth century, but had been rejected. In 1892, the plan of C. Lely (1854-1929) was approved. However, this gigantic project was not begun until 1918 when Lely himself had been appointed Minister of Public Works and his bill for the partial reclamation of this inner sea was passed. Once the Wieringermeer-polder had been drained in

The Philips Competence Centre at Eindhoven, symbol of the technological contributions made by this Dutch multinational

1930, the Zuiderzee was permanently enclosed by the IJsselmeer Dam, completed in 1933. Reclamation of the Northeast-polder was already in progress, but due to the lack of funds work was stopped in the second half of the 'thirties.

Multinationals

Despite widespread social misery, there were some favourable economic developments. The rich sources of raw materials in the Dutch East Indies, and later the strong position of the Netherlands trade and industry on the international market combined to promote the establishment and growth of a number of companies which soon became multinationals – some of them due to the inspiring initiatives of individual entrepreneurs. Among these were the Steenkolen HandelsVereniging (SHV) and the Royal Dutch Petroleum Company, which later merged with the English Shell, as well as, during the 'twenties and 'thirties, Philips. Innovating such traditional Dutch businesses as, for example, dredging and other forms of water control, a few companies in this field gained international recognition as well.

Pacifism and Fascism in the Netherlands between the World Wars

Between the two World Wars, the Netherlands was a loyal member of the recently formed League of Nations, the predecessor of the United Nations. Pacifist ideas dominated the policy of a number of Dutch political parties. Pacifism even led to constitutional revision in 1922, when it was ruled that war could only be declared with the approval of the States-General.
Until a few years before the Second World War, most parties did not give up their pacifist stance. By that time their faith in a peaceful solution of conflicts had been badly shaken both by changes in international relations and by developments at home. Already in the early 'twenties, in the Netherlands, as in the rest of Europe, a number of Fascist and semi-Fascist organizations had appeared. Their members doubted whether parliamentary democracy could survive and they regarded pacifism as useless and even dangerous. One of these organizations, the National Socialist Movement (N.S.B.) joined the political arena. In the 1935 elections the N.S.B. even succeeded in winning almost 8% of the votes. At that time, the N.S.B. was not yet particularly pro-German or anti-Semitic. This changed in later years when the party drifted increasingly into the German camp. The spectacular victory can be explained from the fact that in these years the Dutch economy was at its lowest ebb; this caused many people to feel that a strong man – such as many people thought was in power in Germany – was needed to reorganize politics and the economy and work a way out of the existing misery. Various anti-Fascist movements arose, fully aware of the danger of anti-democratic tendencies. Consequently, the N.S.B. was defeated in the elections of 1937, after which its numbers dwindled rapidly.

Even in 1939, the impulse to remain neutral in foreign policy since the early eighteenth century, held to be the hallmark of the Dutch tradition, coupled to principled pacifism led many to believe that it was necessary to avoid engaging in the war that was so obviously approaching. In August, the King of the Belgians and Queen Wilhelmina offered to mediate between Germany and the other European states. Yet general mobilization was called for in the same month. It was evident that this time the Netherlands would not be able to maintain its neutrality.

Head Office of the Royal Netherlands Petroleum Company in The Hague, built between 1915 and 1917 in neo-renaissance style. The company later merged with the English Shell Oil Company

The interior of the 'Concertgebouw' of Amsterdam, completed in 1888

Culture between the two World Wars

A new movement in the visual arts: 'The Style'

During the first decades of the twentieth century, the Netherlands did participate in the general renewal of cultural life in Europe. Many writers and poets, painters and architects were influenced by the obvious need to rethink old values. The disaster that had been the First World War had taught them that an uncritical continuation of the European tradition would be dangerous. Among the many developments in the arts there was one that gained international interest. It was named after a journal which first appeared in 1917, called 'The Style'. Its founders represented various art forms; for instance, Theo van Doesburg and Piet Mondriaan were painters, while J.J.P. Oud was an architect. The keynote of The Style was to strip art of every unnecessary detail. In architecture this meant that buildings were starkly functional, their structure outlined visibly and without any ornamentation where possible. The most striking and beautiful examples of this are the Hilversum Town Hall, by W.M. Dudok, and the Schröder House in Utrecht, a private dwelling designed by Gerrit Rietveld in 1924 as a three-dimensional plaything of flat planes and colours; it now is open to the public.

Literature

The same moralism as seen in the visual arts was also found in literature. Writers such as Ter Braak, Marsman, Du Perron and Slauerhoff wanted to uphold and pass on the essence and the best of the Dutch tradition by stripping it of false ornament and sentiment. The poets Bloem and Nijhoff were less controversial and polemic, but all authors were aware that this was a time for reflection; consequently, in their works they created a new vitality that even after so many years remains recognisable.

Music

In creative composition, Dutch musicians on the whole did not contribute works of international standard; this may surprise in view of the fact that in these very years the Concertgebouw Orchestra won increasing fame both at home and abroad, especially through its performances of modern music. Since 1920, the conductor, Willem Mengelberg, had earned an international reputation; he laid the foundation for the orchestra's reknown as the ideal performers of the music of such contemporary Dutch composers as Andriessen and Pijper, but predominantly of foreign masters such as Mahler, who was Mengelberg's personal friend, and Richard Strauss.

The mass media

During the first decades of the twentieth century, the new mass media – film, radio and gramophone – made their entry in the Netherlands as well. They soon revolutionized Dutch social life, allowing a far greater group of people to participate in all sorts of culture.
Already in the 'thirties, most families owned a wireless set. They were able to listen to (world) news bulletins, sports commentaries and to music, both popular and classical, that formerly was beyond the means of most; they also listened to the radio plays, which soon became highly popular.
The fact that each of the many broadcasting corporations that were founded represented a specific religious denomination or ideology shows the extent to which the 'pillarization' of Dutch society, its division in groups with their own religious identity, also pervaded cultural life in all its respects. Three of the corporations still operating today were already in action in 1925.

Science

The leading position of the Netherlands as an industrial nation was also reflected in great progress in the sciences and in engineering. In the first decades of the twentieth century, the laboratories of the universities of Leiden and Amsterdam produced many Nobel prize winners. In mathematics, physics and astronomy, Kamerlingh Onnes, Kapteyn, Lorentz and Van der Waals had a world-wide reputation.

Even today Dutch radio and television are organized in many stations, some still based on the original religious 'pillars'

Society and politics during the Second World War

The German occupation: 1940-1945

On May, 10, 1940, German troops invaded the Netherlands. This marked the end of a period of peace which had lasted for over a century. The country had managed to stay out of international conflicts since the struggle with Belgium in 1839 had ended with its separation from the kingdom. But now neutrality could no longer be maintained.
After several days of fighting it was clear that the poorly-equipped Dutch army was no match for the superior strength of the Germans. On May, 13, Queen Wilhelmina and her cabinet ministers left for England unhindered, after foiling German plans to take them prisoner.
A catastrophic and devastating bombardment of Rotterdam and Middelburg followed; when the Germans threatened to destroy other towns if resistance were prolonged, the Dutch army command was forced to capitulate on May, 15.

The persecution of the Jews

Already on May, 29, Arthur Seyss-Inquart took up his position as the German Reich's Commissioner for the Netherlands. It was soon clear that the anti-Semitism displayed by the German government would also be flaunted in the Netherlands. In October 1940 all civil servants had to produce a declaration of Aryan origin. The majority of the population did not yet realize the extent of German anti-Semitism so that many of the declarations were signed. However, it has to be admitted that the Dutch were not free of anti-semitic feelings themselves.
Any hopes that the Jews in this country would not be persecuted were dashed in July 1942. The first groups of Jewish Dutchmen were transported to extermination camps, under the pretext of employment projects in Germany and Poland. In a little over a year 100,000 Jews had been murdered in this way; thus, almost the entire Jewish population of the Netherlands was wiped out. Only a few escaped deportation by going into hiding with Dutch families.
The first resistance organizations were formed at an early stage. For the duration of the war, they were to play an important part in espionage activities and in helping those who, like the Jews, soon realized they had to go into hiding; above all they helped to keep up the morale of the Dutch people, the majority of whom, unlike the members of the N.S.B, did not collaborate with the Germans. From London, Queen Wilhelmina made her own contribution in this respect by encouraging her people in her clandestinely received broadcasts via Radio Orange. As a result, the royal family became a symbol of freedom.

The liberation of the Netherlands: 1944 and 1945

On June, 6, 1944, the allied armies – including Dutch units – landed in Normandy; in the Netherlands, this was followed by "Mad Tuesday", on 5th September. It was started by a rumour that parts of the country had already been liberated by allied soldiers; the rumour was so strong that German troops and numerous members of the N.S.B. hastily left for the eastern frontier.
But another winter passed before the whole of the Netherlands was liberated, a winter of famine that became a traumatic experience for those who managed to live through it. All means of transport had been requisitioned by the Germans so that distribution, especially in the west of the country, came to a virtual standstill; the result was a severe shortage of food everywhere.
When part of the Netherlands was actually

liberated on April, 29, 1945, the first of a series of food parcels was dropped by air and greatly appreciated by the starving population.

The war formally ended for the Netherlands on May, 5, when the Germans signed the capitulation in the presence of Prince Bernhard, the husband of crown princess Juliana. In September 1944, he had assumed command of the so-called Domestic Force; this was a military umbrella organization for all the different resistance groups, which by now often fought amongst themselves.
The return of the royal family – the Queen, Wilhelmina, her only child, the heir to the throne, Juliana, and her three granddaughters – was a sign to all that the war was really over.

Queen Wilhelmina and Princess Juliana: the House of Orange personified after their return from exile

Society, politics and economy after 1945

Post-war housing projects

Clearing the rubble and starting again: new politics and new parties

In the first post-war years the various cabinets could not do much more than to clear away the rubble, to begin with quite literally. Still, during the war ideas had been born and discussed in various socio-political circles that now were put into practice, in the hope of altering the social structure to finally solve some of the worst pre-war problems. Indeed, a number of pre-war situations did not recur. For example, council housing ensured that people with a low income could now move into homes with modern conveniences. Of course this was not achieved in a day, and the housing shortage went on for a very long time. There were also some political parties which did not return after the war. New parties were founded, however, some of them still based on the old ideals of liberalism and socialism but better adapted to the realities of post-war life. These included the Labour Party (PVDA), formed in 1946, the People's

Party for Freedom and Democracy (VVD), formed in 1948, and the Catholic People's Party (KVP), also formed after the war. Two pre-war parties which did return were those based on Protestant principles: the Christian Historical Union and the Anti-Revolutionary Party. In 1976, these two parties merged with the KVP to form the present Christian Democratic Appeal (CDA).

International co-operation and integration

As a small country that had suffered greatly from the war between the European states, the Netherlands were eager indeed to join international consultative bodies. From the start in 1945, it was a member of the United Nations. In 1947 already, a customs' union was formed with Belgium and Luxembourg, which was consolidated in the so-called Benelux in 1948. The Netherlands has also belonged to NATO from the first. The European Community has always had the wholehearted support of the Dutch, maybe not because they actually wished to create a pan-European community but in the hope that their ideals regarding their own society would be upheld and strengthened, especially by the advantages of economic and political co-operation.

The Dutch East Indies declares its independence: Indonesia is born

The colonies – which had been renamed 'overseas territories' in the constitutional revision of 1922 – became independent, or partially so, after the war. In the case of the Dutch East Indies this was preceded by an unsuccessful Dutch military campaign. Immediately following the capitulation of Japan, which had occupied the Dutch East Indies for almost four years, indigenous political groups had declared the independence of 'Indonesia'. The Netherlands' government then considered granting independence to 'the United States of Indonesia', but within the context of the Dutch kingdom. In 1946, an agreement to this effect was signed between the Netherlands and the Republic of Indonesia at Lingadjati. The Republic, which dominated Sumatra and Java, wanted to extend its powers to the other parts of the archipelago, which for a number of reasons did not welcome this development. In the ensuing confusion, the first 'police actions' were carried out by the Dutch government in 1947, when Dutch troops tried, in vain, to protect the interests of these other regions, as well as in the hope that the construction of a 'united kingdom' could be retained. After a second campaign in 1949, a round-table conference was held at The Hague; partly due to international pressure, on December, 27, of that year a transfer of sovereignty took place, whereby the Republic of Indonesia was given the freedom to try and gain command of the whole archipelago.

The Charter of the Kingdom is granted to the former colonies in the West

There had already been a round-table conference between the Netherlands, Surinam and the Netherlands Antilles in 1948. After a third conference in 1954, the Charter of the Kingdom was declared, granting these overseas territories in the West far-reaching independence. Surinam became completely autonomous in 1975. A similar freedom has been offered to the islands of the Netherlands Antilles but has not been accepted by them, yet.

The House of Orange

To Queen Wilhelmina, the post-war period in the Netherlands was a disappointment. During the war she had developed ideas about an ideal, strongly coherent society. But the highly varied and to her confusing reality of politics in the years following the war did not live up to this. In 1948, after having celebrated her fiftieth anniversary on the throne, she abdicated in favour of her

The 1949 transfer of Dutch sovereignty over Indonesia to the new Republic (Anefo)

daughter Juliana.
More than fifty years later, the place of the sovereign is still filled by a member of the House of Orange. In 1980, Queen Juliana in her turn abdicated in favour of her eldest daughter, since when Queen Beatrix has symbolized the unity of the people of the Netherlands in her own way.

The Delta project accomplished

During the second part of the twentieth century, a great deal of work has been done in civil engineering. Many motorways have been built, to accommodate a growing number of cars. The Zuider Zee-project was continued with the reclamation of eastern and southern Flevoland. The debate concerning the reclamation of the western part known as Markerwaard is still going on.
An even greater project of the former sea, realized over the past decades, was the Delta plan, designed following a result of a disastrous storm which flooded the islands of Zeeland in 1953, at the cost of 1835 lives. The project protects the low-lying areas of the south-western Netherlands against the sea. A start was made in 1957 when all the Zeeland inlets were sealed off. The storm-surge barrier in the Eastern Scheldt was brought into operation by Queen Beatrix in 1986. This gigantic feat of engineering had taken almost thirty years to complete; together with the Zuider Zee-project, it established the Netherlands' world-wide reputation in this field.

Economic boom and recession: social legislation and social problems

After the war, many people were unable or unwilling to wait for the economy to recover; they decided to emigrate. At the beginning of the 'fifties hundreds of thousands of people left the country. This time their major destinations were Australia, Canada and New Zealand. In the same period a wave of immigrants arrived from the Dutch East Indies, to be followed later by a steady stream of over 400.000 people from Surinam and the Antillies.

Meanwhile, there was work to be done in the Netherlands; in this, the people, like all over western Europe, were stimulated by the American Marshall Plan, that provided a major economic and financial injection. Food rationing was lifted in 1949 and there were several rounds of wage increases of 5% at a time to raise the standard of living. This policy, coupled with fresh investments, expanding industries and strongly increasing exports, boosted the economy towards the end of the 'fifties. As a result, the Dutch economy, though prospering, became more sensitive to global fluctuations.
In the 'sixties', there was something of a boom, partly due to Dutch membership of the European Economic Community which the Netherlands had joined in 1957. This continued until well into the 'seventies when the international economic crisis made itself felt all over Europe.
Meanwhile, the growing prosperity of the Netherlands was being translated into a national social policy. In this respect, the name of one of the greatest post-war politicians, Dr. Willem Drees (1886 -1988) has to be mentioned. He was Minister of Social Affairs in the first two post-war cabinets; in that period he provided for special legislation to take care of the old-age pensioners. Between 1948 and 1958, he headed four coalitions, that gathered all the big parties. The social security system, forming the basis of the much-admired and much-maligned

◀ *Portrait of Queen Beatrix on the occasion of her inauguration in 1980 (RVD The Hague)*

The Eastern Scheldt storm-surge barrier is part of the Delta project to safeguard the islands of Zeeland against the water ▶

S1
S1

Dutch 'welfare state', has its roots in this period. The system was not put to the test during the years of affluence. Unemployment figures had fallen so sharply that it was considered necessary to take in immigrant labourers from Italy, Greece, Spain and later also from Morocco and Turkey. Many of these workers settled permanently in the Netherlands.

With the immigrants from Surinam and the Antilles, this development has made the Netherlands into a veritable multicultural society. The government is asked to enable all minority groups to uphold their own cultural values, but it is also essential that the groups concerned are assimilated in Dutch society and culture. Constitutional reform has since granted foreign workers the right to take part in municipal elections.

However, when economic decline reached a climax in the 'eighties, the social security system was put to the test; its partial demolition since has led to social and political tension. During the period of affluence between 1960 and 1974 there had been a tendency to look for new ideals, especially among the young. Now, their efforts are once more concentrated on ordering their lives and futures as comfortably as possible. With the employment situation fluctuating since the 'eighties, and social services being less generous, the average Dutch person is intent on finding and holding on to a job. This leaves little time for flamboyant social criticism. The situation also is reflected in foreign policy, that had been dominated by a longing for peace in the first decades following the war. In the 'sixties and 'seventies, many of the Dutch could see no sense in the arms' race between the western and eastern parts of Europe, and huge protest demonstrations were organized to express their revulsion against the use of nuclear weapons. Particularly among leftists, this pacifist attitude sometimes became violently anti-American. Since the disarmament talks between Russia and America and especially since the fall of communism in Eastern Europe in 1989 and 1990, political awareness has been far less active. During the last decades of the twentieth century, involvement in the serious problems facing society seems to have grown less intense, too, probably due to individual concern over economic well-being.

Culture after 1960

Education in the Netherlands has been entirely re-organized since the war, starting with the 'Mammoth Act' regulating secondary education that was passed in 1963 and implemented in 1968. This Act was to promote the mobility of one type of education to another, especially for the benefit of those social groups which traditionally were not readily admitted to higher education. The Primary Education Act implemented in 1985 did away with the distinction between the infant and primary schools, bringing the school age down to 5 years. The reorganization of higher education in the 'eighties led to cuts in the length of university studies, and to mergers between the various forms of vocational training. The underlying question whether education is the most efficient instrument to effectuate social change, and realize equality of opportunities, still remains unanswered.

One of the most creative post-war artistic movements in the Netherlands – the abstract art produced by members of the Cobra group – became internationally famous, especially through the work of Karel Appel.
In literature, the 'Men of the 'Fifties' included Lucebert and Remco Campert, both of whom wrote experimental poetry. The prose writer Van 't Reve also broke with tradition; he established his fame with a novel, *The Evenings*, that was the perfect evocation of life following the war, of the sober years of reconstruction and the sense that changes should occur.
It is a fact that after the Second World War

there was a general longing for a break-through to more freedom of expression in the various fields of culture, unhampered by a tradition that according to many had only led to a fiasco. Was not this the lesson World War II had taught? These feelings seem reminiscent of the mood in the period after World War I.
Part of this mood undoubtedly resulted in greater freedom in the fields of sexual life and emotion – enhancing drugs' use; many uninformed foreigners now allow an exaggerated vision of these aspects to colour their view of Dutch culture. Part of cultural development in the widest sense was that the barriers between the traditional socio-religious 'compartments' or 'pillars' were breaking down; it is increasingly obvious that culture and society cannot be kept anymore within the confines of religious and ideological subgroups. The churches are empty, and the Churches are losing their members. But the loss of tradition and of the socio-cultural framework that used to provide a sense of security, sometimes seems to make people long for old ideas and movements, which now are being eclectically recombined to provide new meanings, as can be seen in the great popularity of all sorts of 'New Age'-ideas and ideologies. Obviously, a new culture is taking shape, that may be 'global' while retaining a number of Dutch characteristics in its continued sense of controlled freedom.

Bridge opened in 1996, connecting the two parts of Rotterdam separated by the River Maas

Conclusion

It would not do to end a historical survey with predictions for the future. But it seems fitting to point out that, generally speaking, at the turn of the millennium the Dutch people have developed a clearly-defined idea of their culture and society. Formed in the past, this self-knowledge serves as a guideline for life in the present, and may do so, too, for the unforeseeable future.

A small nation which likes to think of itself as both tolerant and cosmopolitan. The coming decades will reveal whether this – smug? – image resembles reality.

A small country which is apt to boast from time to time. Won from the water, formerly one of the leading commercial powers in the world, it is still one of its most highly industrialized societies. It has also endeavoured to attain a high standard of social justice. The coming decades will reveal whether these achievements can stand the test of time.

A small state which is prepared to relinquish some of the traditional elements of sovereignty and independence to promote welfare and well-being in a broader, European setting. In this respect, too, the next decades will reveal whether this policy bears fruit.

In short, the Netherlands likes to think of itself as taking the lead, both in Europe and the world. This incurs both admiration and irritation, because as a nation, it remains 'small among the great'.

A vision of the future? A multi-cultural, global society, within the context of one of the Netherlands' oldest towns ▶

HOTEL
AMUSEMENT
利口福
CHOPSTIX
DAMHOTEL
Nikon
HOTEL
DELTA
HOTEL
Marlboro
HOTEL
Pizzeria
KING KONG
CAMERA'S
HOTEL
SONY
16
753

CHRONOLOGICAL OUTLINE

	Prehistory
c. 10,000 B.C.	The last ice ages
c. 1900-750 B.C.	The bronze age
c. 750 B.C.	The iron age
57 B.C. – A.D. 406	*Roman rule*
until c. 650	Germanic society Saxons, Frisians, Franks. Conversion to Christianity
c. 650 – 850	*The Carolingian Empire*
800-814	Charlemagne
c. 850-1000	The Norsemen
c. 1000	The development of territorial principalities. Regional sovereignty
c. 1200	The towns set the tone in politics, economy and culture
1350 – 1581	*Burgundian-Hapsburg rule*
	Centralization of power and authority
	The Reformation
1515-1555	Charles V
1555-1581	Philip II
1586 – 1648	*The 'Eighty Years' War'; Rebellion against foreign rule*
1576	The Pacification of Gent
1579	The Union of Atrecht and the Union of Utrecht
1581	*The Act of Abjuration*
1581	Actual establishment of 'The Republic of the Seven United Provinces'
1648	The Peace of Münster: formal recognition of the Dutch Republic
17th century	*The 'Dutch Golden Age'.*
	Voyages of discovery.
1602 and 1621	Establishment of United East India Company and West India Company

18th century	*The Republic politically a second-rate power.*
1747	Oranges hereditary stadhouders
	Patriots and Orangists
1795-1806	*The Batavian Republic and its aftermath*
1806-1810	King Louis Napoleon
1810-1813	The French Period
1814-1830/39	*The Kingdom of the United Netherlands*
1814-1840	King William I
1830	Establishment of the Belgian State
1839-	*The Kingdom of the Netherlands*
1840-1849	King William II
1849-1890	King William III
1890-1948	Queen Wilhelmina
1948-1980	Queen Juliana
1980-	Queen Beatrix
1840 and 1848	Constitutional revisions
1840-1890	Towards an industrial society: phase I
1890-1945	Towards an industrial society: phase II
1914-1940	Policy of neutrality. Pacifism
1914-1918	World War I
	Economic crisis
	Fascism.
1940-1945	The German occupation during World War II
1945-c. 1960	*Reconstruction.*
	International Co-operation
c. 1960-c. 1980	Economic boom; the 'welfare state'.
c. 1980-	Further European integration.
	Quest for an equilibrium in a social and multicultural society

Simplified family tree of the House of Orange-Nassau

Jan V Count of Nassau (1455-1516)

Henry III of Nassau (1483-1538)

René of Chalons,
Prince of Orange
(1519-1544),
died without issue

William 'the Rich' (1487-1559)

first line

William I of Nassau
(1533-1584),
inherits title Prince
of Orange 1544

Maurice (1567-1625)
stadhouder (1585-1625)

Frederick Henry (1584-1647)
stadhouder (1625-1647)

William II (1626-1650)
stadhouder (1647-1650)

William III (1650-1702)
stadhouder (1672-1702)
King of England (1689-1702)
First line Orange Nassau
becomes extinct 1702

Albertine Agnes (1634-1696)

X

William Frederick
of Nassau-Dietz (1613-1664)
stadhouder of Friesland (1640-1664)

second line

Jan VI 'the Elder' (1536-1606)
Count of Nassau-Siegen etc.

Ernest Casimir (1573-1632)
ancestor Nassau-Dietz line;
stadhouder of Friesland
(1620-1632)

William Frederick (1613-1664)
stadhouder of Friesland
(1640-1664)

Henry Casimir II (1657-1696)
stadhouder of Friesland
(1664-1696)

John William Friso (1687-1711)
prince of Orange from 1702 stad-
houder of Friesland (1696-1711)

William IV (1711-1751)
stadhouder of Friesland (1711)
hereditary stadhouder of all the
provinces (1747-1751)

William V (1748-1806)
hereditary stadhouder of all the
provinces (1751-1795)

William I (1772-1843)
sovereign ruler (1813-1815)
King of the Netherlands (1815-
1840) Grand Duke of
Luxembourg (1815-1843)

William II (1792-1849)
King of the Netherlands (1840-
1849) Grand Duke of
Luxembourg (1840-1849)

William III (1817-1890)
King of the Netherlands (1849-
1890) Grand Duke of Luxem-
bourg (1849-1890) As William
died without male heirs,
Luxembourg fell to a collateral
branch of the Nassau family.

Wilhelmina (1880-1962)
Queen of the Netherlands (1890-
1948)

Juliana (1909-)
Queen of the Netherlands (1948-
1980)

Beatrix (1938-)
Queen of the Netherlands (1980-)

William Alexander (1986-), heir
to the throne.

first line Orange Nassau

second line Orange Nassau